Praise for
The Politics of Witness

Anyone who thinks the church isn't political doesn't understand that the church is a politic; and anyone who doesn't think the gospel is political hasn't come to terms with the fundamental claim that Jesus is Lord. Allan Bevere, an ecclesial theologian, combines in this book a wonderful "church as politics" with gospel in a wise, warm and challenging manner.

Scot McKnight
Karl A. Olsson Professor in Religious Studies
North Park University

Allan Bevere has written a timely, eye-opening, and thought-provoking book for Christians, whether they consider themselves conservative or progressive. He calls us all to forsake the seductive, insidious error of Christendom and civil religion in order to follow Jesus and bear witness to the reign of God. May this book contribute to the renewal of the church for the sake of the world and the glory of God.

Michael J. Gorman
Professor of Sacred Scripture and Dean, The Ecumenical
Institute of Theology
St. Mary's Seminary & University, Baltimore, Maryland

The Church has tragically returned again and again to the mistake of equating the progress of God's kingdom with the acquisition of temporal political power. Allan Bevere skillfully demonstrates that the modern religious right and left are equally attracted to this error. He calls the Church back to its mission of incarnating the alternative *polis* that is God's true kingdom -- a necessary corrective for all Christians in times of heated rhetoric and increasing civil strife.

David W. Opderbeck
Associate Professor of Law
Seton Hall University

Allan R. Bevere is a pastor with the West Akron Regional Ministry of the United Methodist Church (Akron, Ohio) and a Professional Fellow in Theology at Ashland Theological Seminary (Ashland, Ohio). He received his Ph.D from the University of Durham, U.K. He has written three books, *The Character of Our Discontent, Sharing in the Inheritance: Identity and the Moral Life in Colossians* and *All Is Not As It Seems: Random Reflections on Faith, Ethics, and Politics,* and is currently working on several more. He has published sermons, contributed articles to a Bible Dictionary, and most recently contributed a chapter to *Jesus and Paul: Global Perspectives in Honor of James D. G. Dunn for His 70th Birthday.* Bevere engages in a teaching mission in Cuba with the United Methodist Church. He is married and has four children.

The *Areopagus Critical Christian Issues* series examines important issues in understanding Christian beliefs and developing sound Christian practice. Each booklet is short — less than 80 pages in length — and provides an academically sound and biblically rooted examination of a particular question about doctrine or practice or an area of basic Christian belief. It is jointly edited by Dr. Allan R. Bevere and Dr. David Alan Black.

The Politics of Witness
The Character of the Church
in the World

Allan R. Bevere

Energion Publications
P. O. Box 841
Gonzalez, FL 32560

www.energionpubs.com

2011

ISBN10: 1-893729-81-8
ISBN13: 978-1893729-81-0
Library of Congress Control Number: 2011931389

In honor and in memory of
Archie Penner (1917-2007)
who first challenged me to rethink Christendom
and a status quo ecclesiology.

Table of Contents

Acknowledgments..ix

Preface: The Zigzags of a Journey.. xi

1 Introduction:

The Central and All-Encompassing Dilemma..........................1

2 Jesus and the Reconstitution of Israel:

The Church as Chosen Nation...5

3 The Constantinian Shift:

A (Not So) Funny Thing Happened on the Way to Rome..17

4 Constantine's Modern Lieutenants:

Thomas Jefferson and Benjamin Franklin...............................27

5 It's Israel and the Church, Not Israel and America:

An Ecclesial Hermeneutic...37

6 Why the Church in America Cannot Speak Truth to Power. 43

7 The Politics of Witness:

A (Not So) Modest Proposal..51

For Further Reading..63

Topics and Persons Index.. 67

Scripture Index...71

From the Editors

The Areopagus is a hill in Athens that was once the meeting place of a Greek council. Paul preached on that hill while visiting Athens, presenting the gospel to the Athenian council and converting one of them (Acts 17). It thus provides an excellent name for this series of booklets that examines important issues in understanding Christian beliefs and developing sound Christian practice. Each booklet is intentionally short – less than 80 pages in length – and provides an academically sound and biblically rooted examination of a particular question about doctrine or practice or an area of basic Christian belief.

The Areopagus series is orthodox in doctrine but not bound to the doctrinal statements of any denomination. It is both firm in conviction and irenic in tone. Authors have been chosen for their ability to understand a topic in depth and present it clearly.

Each book is rigorous in scholarship because we believe the church deserves no less. Yet the volumes are accessible in style as we also believe that there are many pastors and laypersons in the church who desire to think deeply and critically about the issues that confront the church today in its life and mission in the world.

In keeping with these convictions, the authors in this series are either professors who are also actively involved in ministry, pastors who have not only thought through the issues but whose ministry has been guided by their convictions, or laypersons whose faith and commitment to the lordship of Jesus Christ and his church have contributed to the Great Commission Jesus gave to all of his followers (Matt. 28:18-20).

The *Areopagus Critical Christian Issues* series is not only meant to help the church think differently. We hope that those who read its volumes will be different, for the gospel is about the transformation of the whole person – mind, heart, and soul.

We take the words of the apostle Paul seriously when he says to the Athenians that God "has fixed a day on which he will have the world judged in righteousness by a man whom he has appointed; and of this he has given assurance to all by raising him from the dead" (Acts 17:31).

Allan R. Bevere
David Alan Black
Editors

Acknowledgments

Whenever I write acknowledgements for a book, I am reminded that there not only is not enough space to thank all of those who make something like this possible, but there is not enough clarity of memory in my brain to remember everyone. So like all acknowledgements, this one will be quite selective.

I certainly must thank Henry Neufeld and Energion Publications. I cannot overemphasize what a great joy and privilege it has been to work with Henry on various projects, and I appreciate his patience with me as I attempt to balance more responsibilities than one human being should be allowed to have.

I also express my gratitude to my co-editor for the Areopagus Series, Dave Black. Prior to my time with Energion, I only knew Dave by name. It is a gift to now know him personally, and it is a pleasure to work with him as a colleague.

Of course, I cannot begin to state in words the love and support of my family. My wife Carol continues to encourage me as a pastor and a professor, a short-term missionary, a (former) police chaplain, and a writer. She probably wonders at times what is coming next, but I have never had to wonder about her love for me. Such love is a wonderful gift that I receive daily.

Then there are our four children: Alyssa, Courtney, Joshua, and Jason. It is not possible to imagine life without them. Children are indeed a gift from God and we have been blessed four-fold. I think they are somewhat impressed that I am a writer, but what I want them to see in me more than anything else is a Dad whose life is greatly blessed by their presence.

Finally, I wish to thank all my discussion partners on this subject, whether they come in written form or over discussion and coffee. I want to make special mention of James Hunter whose work I draw on rather heavily in chapters five and six. I was thinking about these issues long before Hunter published his recent book, *To Change the World*, but I know of no one who has articulated the subject matter better than he has.

I do not know how I would think about these all-important subjects without such fellow travelers along the intellectual way. They sustain me as one who probably thinks too hard about too many things.

Epiphany 2011

Preface

The Zigzags of a Journey

Two roads diverged in a wood, and I – I took the one less traveled by, and that has made all the difference.-- Robert Frost

The subject of this book is of extreme importance to me. Of course, any subject on which an author writes should be significant to him or her. But this particular subject—the politics of witness— is one that has totally reoriented my outlook and perspective on the Christian life, on Christian discipleship.

The position I put forward in this small book is not a view I have always embraced. I grew up in a typical devout Christian household—a household that never questioned that we were mired in Christendom. Indeed, we never thought about Christendom since we did not know there were other options. Throughout my close to half a century journey in this life, I have been a Republican, I have been a Democrat, I have been a political activist (in both Sojourners and Focus on the Family-like fashion), and at one point I was sure the Amish had it right in complete withdrawal from the larger happenings in the world. But the more I read Scripture and the more I read such thinkers as John Howard Yoder, Stanley Hauerwas, Jacques Ellul, William Stringfellow, and others, the more I began to see the decisive inadequacies of the aforementioned political possibilities. I came to the point in my life where I could no longer embrace Christendom as a viable option for Christians. So for the next few years, I thought it would be possible to reform it. But I soon discovered that those who attempt to reform Christendom end up getting reformed by it. Indeed, I would even use the word "converted." It was only after a long journey of zigzagging through "this position" and "that perspective" that I came to the realization that the only possible response of the

Christian toward Christendom was its rejection (as articulated very well by Carter, *Rethinking Christ and Culture*, pp. 77-93). This book is about the rejection of Christendom. Until Christendom is abandoned by Christians, the church's mission and witness in the world will be seriously undermined.

There are two major flaws in this book. I know that is hardly a way to entice a reader into going further, but in actuality I think these two flaws are the book's greatest strengths. By the time you, the reader, finish with the last page, I hope you will agree.

The first flaw is that I have I have tried to deal with too much material in too little space. The subjects of chapters two through seven need more detail and explication. There is no doubt that those who critique this work will raise questions as to the matters I failed to deal with sufficiently as well as the issues I completely ignored. But that is precisely a strength, for each chapter contains indispensable material for the subject of the politics of witness. This little book is the beginning of a dialogue on an extremely important matter—the character of the church in the world. It is a discussion that has been taking place for two thousand years to be sure. So in one obvious sense this book is not a beginning. But what I believe is new or at least newly emphasized is the way I consistently frame the matters of concern. While the subject of the church's witness has hardly been ignored, I have overtly tied the church's witness to politics and politics to ecclesiology. In this book I ask the church to consider the recovery of a robust political ecclesiology that sees the very life and witness of the *ecclesia* as its politics, and that the primary and central political posture of the church toward the nations is not one of influence in the political chambers of Washington D.C., but by embodying in its collective life what God expects of the nations.

As reviewers critique my work, it is my hope that they will raise questions, not only for further discussion, but for further revision of this work. It is my hope and desire, at some point, to expand upon each chapter eventually publishing a larger and fuller treatment. That larger work cannot be written without the affirmation and critique of the *ecclesia*l community. I look forward to that discussion.

The second flaw is that it is not completely clear whether the following chapters constitute something connected with one another as should be the case with a monograph, or whether each chapter is more of an essay in a small anthology. I will say only this: While the connections between chapters may not be as tight as one would expect in a monograph, they nevertheless come to focus on a single theme—that the church can only reclaim its mission and prophetic witness in the world by embracing the politics of witness.

I need to make one important comment of clarification: This manuscript was finished and went into production before the publication of Peter Leithart's fine book, *Defending Constantine: The Twilight of an Empire and the Dawn of Christendom*. Thus I was not able to consult the work. I have however, read it since. What I can say in response to Leithart's critique of John Howard Yoder's critique of Constantine is that while Leithart's argument that Yoder misunderstood Constantine the man is largely correct, Yoder still gets Constantinianism and its deleterious effects by and large correct. Thus Yoder remains one of the most significant individuals for understanding that period of church history and its implications for today.

I freely admit that the road I have taken in this book is not the road taken by the majority of Christians. Some will no doubt conclude that such minority status already demonstrates that I and those few who are like-minded are wrong. I will only say in response that not only is the majority not always right, but stagnant group-think is more often the product of many people than of only a few. In this book I seek a way out of a status quo ecclesiology and a completely uninteresting understanding of nation state politics. In any case, I hope those who work through these pages will do so with an open mind willing to consider that perhaps God is looking for a remnant to faithfully embody the politics of witness to the nations.

A statement you will find in several places throughout this book is a favorite quote of mine from Stanley Hauerwas: "It is God and not the nations who rules the world." That is the claim I wish to assert throughout because I believe that while most Christians believe the truth of that claim, they do so only in the abstract. Functionally, by the church's political engagements and by aligning themselves with the left and the right, Democrats and Republicans, Christians in actuality betray the unacknowledged belief that it is the nations that are indeed running the show. I wish to challenge that unacknowledged belief in no uncertain terms.

1
Introduction:
The Central and
All-Encompassing Dilemma

The church did not prevent the two world wars, and could not prevent them. They simply broke over it. But what is disturbing today is something beyond the mere fact of the two wars: the church is the body of Christ, beyond all boundaries, the people of God among the nations. That in 1914 Christians went enthusiastically to war against Christians, baptized against baptized, was not seen in any way as a destruction of what the church is in and of its very nature, a destruction that cried out to heaven. That was the real catastrophe. — Gerhard Lohfink.

The church's most significant dilemma that it faces at the dawn of the twenty-first century is the same dilemma it has faced since the fourth century: What to do with Constantinianism and what to do with Christendom? In facing this most difficult challenge the very character of the church is at stake, the very character of its mission is in jeopardy. While the vast majority of believers have embraced Constantinianism (the belief that Christians should forge a close alliance with the state in order to influence and, if possible, enact Christian policies) and Christendom (the product of Constantinianism where the culture of a nation reflects Christianity and vestiges of Christian values), I believe that Christians must reject both if they are to be faithful witnesses to the gospel in the world.

It is from the ministry of Jesus that we understand how Jesus intended to reconstitute the nation of Israel in his ministry. In gathering twelve disciples around him, Jesus was founding a nation (that would become known as "Church") that would uniquely bear witness to the nations of the ways of the Lord; and the ways of this holy nation would not be the ways of the nations of the world (chapter 2).

But some two hundred and fifty years after Jesus, the church would be confronted with its greatest temptation—the temptation to wield power, to reject Jesus' upside down kingdom and replace it with the typical status quo model of the pagans. The Emperor Constantine would offer the church such a temptation, and it would find itself unable to resist (chapter 3).

Many centuries later, Enlightenment thinkers such as Thomas Jefferson and Ben Franklin wanted to get the church out of the political power brokering business. They did so by positing faith and doctrine as nothing more than a matter of personal preference—irrelevant for the hard and difficult questions of politics and statecraft. For these men the public value of religion was to be found only in its morals, the status quo morals of good citizenship. In attempting to rid the modern world of the Constantinian practice of church and nation ruling in an alliance side by side, they ironically reinforced the church as nothing more than an institution to be used to further the state's agenda. Thomas Jefferson and Ben Franklin thus become Constantine's unwitting lieutenants (chapter 4).

Of course none of this would be possible without reference to Scripture. Both the religious right and the religious left in the twentieth and twenty-first centuries have resorted to a faulty hermeneutic in order to further their agendas that place the nation state at the center of politics instead of the church. They do this quite freely and without reflecting deeply upon how they are misusing Scripture. Both sides take passages of Scripture that clearly refer either to Israel or the church and apply them directly to the nation state. It is this flawed method of biblical interpretation that marginalizes the church, thus replacing it with the nation state, which is now elevated to divinely approved status (chapter 5).

All of this means that the church in the modern West is unable to effectively speak truth to power (to turn a phrase popular with some today). The reason is that since Christians have embraced the power politics of the nation state and have chosen up sides as

Republicans or Democrats, conservatives or liberals, the church cannot be a prophetic witness because it has been compromised and has a stake in the very power it is supposed to challenge (chapter 6).

What this means, finally, is that the church must exorcize the ghost of Constantine from its midst and bury Christendom with the relics of a long and unfortunate past. The church must recover its unique character as an alternative to the world by bearing witness in its collective life to the ways of God. The church must embrace the politics of the kingdom by being itself. Only then can the nations come to understand that it is God and not the nations who rules the world.

2
Jesus and the Reconstitution of Israel: The Church as Chosen Nation

...when Jesus first gave what we now call the Sermon on the Mount, he was staging something that would look to us much more like a political rally. He was like someone drumming up support for a new movement, a new great cause. He was calling his hearers, quite simply, to a new way of being Israel, a new way of being God's people for the world. — N.T. Wright

There are only two nations in human history called directly into existence by God—Israel and the church. Our focus throughout the book is the church, but we cannot understand what it means for the church to be God's nation of people called into existence by him without first knowing how Israel is called of God to be God's people in the world.

THE LIGHT TO THE NATIONS

The story of Israel begins in Genesis 12 with the calling of Abraham:

Now the LORD said to Abram, "Go from your country and your kindred and your father's house to the land that I will show you. I will make of you a great nation, and I will bless you, and make your name great, so that you will be a blessing. I will bless those who bless you, and the one who curses you I will curse; and in you all the families of the earth shall be blessed."

So Abram went, as the LORD had told him; and Lot went with him. Abram was seventy-five years old when he departed from Haran. Abram took his wife Sarai and his brother's son Lot, and all the possessions that they had gathered, and the persons whom they had acquired in Haran; and they set forth to go to the land of

Canaan. When they had come to the land of Canaan, Abram passed through the land to the place at Shechem, to the oak of Moreh. At that time the Canaanites were in the land. Then the LORD *appeared to Abram, and said, "To your offspring I will give this land." So he built there an altar to the* LORD, *who had appeared to him. From there he moved on to the hill country on the east of Bethel, and pitched his tent, with Bethel on the west and Ai on the east; and there he built an altar to the* LORD *and invoked the name of the* LORD. *And Abram journeyed on by stages towards the Negeb* (Genesis 12:1-9).

Abraham is not told the purpose of his calling to be the father of a great nation; he is only told to go where God leads. Even though Abraham has no idea how God is going to fulfill his promise, he nevertheless steps out in faith in his old age and takes himself and his family and all of his possessions to a new land that God has given to him (see Bevere, *The Character of Our Discontent*, 5).

The purpose of Israel's calling becomes clear in the later Old Testament narrative. In the latter chapters of Isaiah, likely written some 1300-1500 years after Abraham, the prophet reminds Israel of her high calling to bear witness to the other nations that their God is indeed the one, true God.

Listen to me, you that pursue righteousness, you that seek the LORD. *Look to the rock from which you were hewn, and to the quarry from which you were dug.* ²*Look to Abraham your father and to Sarah who bore you; for he was but one when I called him, but I blessed him and made him many.* ³*For the* LORD *will comfort Zion; he will comfort all her waste places, and will make her wilderness like Eden, her desert like the garden of the* LORD; *joy and gladness will be found in her thanksgiving and the voice of song.*

⁴*Listen to me, my people, and give heed to me, my nation; for a teaching will go out from me, and my justice for a light to the peoples.* ⁵*I will bring near my deliverance swiftly, my salvation*

has gone out and my arms will rule the peoples; the coastlands wait for me, and for my arm they hope (Isaiah 51:1-6).

It is important to notice that the prophet reminds Israel of the beginnings of her calling in reference to Abraham and Sarah. It is Israel's return from exile that will bear witness to the justice of God. It will be a light to the nations, and Israel will reflect that light to the peoples who surround her. Israel as God's light is specifically made clear in Isaiah 60.

> *Arise, shine; for your light has come, and the glory of the LORD has risen upon you. For darkness shall cover the earth, and thick darkness the peoples; but the LORD will arise upon you, and his glory will appear over you. Nations shall come to your light, and kings to the brightness of your dawn.*

> *Lift up your eyes and look around; they all gather together, they come to you; your sons shall come from far away, and your daughters shall be carried on their nurses' arms. Then you shall see and be radiant; your heart shall thrill and rejoice, because the abundance of the sea shall be brought to you, the wealth of the nations shall come to you* (Isaiah 60:1-5).

The nation will reflect the glory of the Lord; their very existence will witness to the existence and the character of their God. "God's call of Israel to be his people, to live under his rule, was itself designed as the central move in putting the world to rights." It is through Israel that God will "put the world to rights" (N.T. Wright, *The Last Word,* p. 35).

Of course, if Israel was to bear faithful witness to the character of their God, then Israel must bear that very same character. The Prophet Jeremiah has some clear and decisive words to his own people for their lack of faithfulness. They are unable to bear witness to the nations because they have become like the nations.

"If you will return, O Israel, return to me," declares the LORD. "If you put your detestable idols out of my sight and no longer go astray, and if in a truthful, just and righteous way you swear, 'As surely as the LORD lives,' then the nations will be blessed by him and in him they will glory."

This is what the LORD says to the men of Judah and to Jerusalem: "Break up your unplowed ground and do not sow among thorns. Circumcise yourselves to the LORD, circumcise your hearts, you men of Judah and people of Jerusalem, or my wrath will break out and burn like fire because of the evil you have done-- burn with no one to quench it (Jeremiah 4:1-4).

The command for the Israelites to circumcise their hearts is significant. It was the Law of Moses that specifically marked Israel as the people of God in the world (see Bevere, *Sharing in the Inheritance*, pp. 53-121). It was their worship of the one true God and obedience to the covenant that actualized Israel's witness in the world. When Israel fell into idolatry and worshiped other deities and when they failed to obey the covenant, they were no longer reflecting their place as distinctive from the nations of the world; they were acting like all the other nations of the world. In other words, even though the Israelite males were circumcised, the most important sign of the covenant, they were behaving as the uncircumcised nations surrounding the people of God. Thus, Jeremiah is saying that the physical mark of circumcision is not enough to be the people of God. A way of life in keeping with the character of God's people is also necessary. If the life of God's people Israel cannot be distinguished from the way of life exhibited by the other nations, then Israel has no witness to the world.

And that is the central point, as we will see shortly when we get to the ministry of Jesus. The nation of Israel was created for a purpose. Long before Abraham's birth, God was planning to redeem the world, and Israel was to be the vehicle by which that redemption would be proclaimed and embodied. Israel was called out by God from among the nations, not to be isolated from the

Gentiles, but to model for the nations what God desired of them. It was absolutely essential, therefore, that God's people keep the covenant, not only for their own sake, but for the sake of the world. Israel existed for the sake of the world.

The problem, however, was not only idolatry and the trampling of the covenant, but the attitude later on in Israel's history that what it meant to be the people of God was primarily a privilege, not a responsibility. There were some Jews who came to see their chosen status as more of a statement as to how special they were as God's people, better than everyone else, instead of understanding their calling as a claim as to how much God cared for the entire world—Jew and Gentile as well.

We see this tension between chosenness as a privilege versus a responsibility playing out in the Old Testament itself. The Book of Ezra represents the point of view of exclusion of the Gentiles for the sake of maintaining the ethnic and therefore covenantal purity of the people of God (see LaSor *et al*, *Old Testament Survey*, p. 656). During the exile the Jews were convinced that their Babylonian captivity was the direct result of their failure to keep the covenant as explicated in the Law of Moses. They had compromised with paganism, just like King Ahab who married the foreign Queen Jezebel. Ahab became the epitome of Jewish compromise and Jezebel had come to be seen as the exemplification of the kind of paganism that Israel could not tolerate. Even ethnically mixed marriages were suspect because of the fear that paganism would be reintroduced into a post-exilic Jewish population. Ezra speaks of the problem:

After these things had been done, the officials approached me and said, 'The people of Israel, the priests, and the Levites have not separated themselves from the peoples of the lands with their abominations, from the Canaanites, the Hittites, the Perizzites, the Jebusites, the Ammonites, the Moabites, the Egyptians, and the Amorites. ²For they have taken some of their daughters as wives for themselves and for their sons. Thus the holy seed has mixed itself with the peoples of the lands, and in this faithlessness the

*officials and leaders have led the way.' ³When I heard this, I tore
my garment and my mantle, and pulled hair from my head and
beard, and sat appalled. ⁴Then all who trembled at the words of
the God of Israel, because of the faithlessness of the returned
exiles, gathered around me while I sat appalled until the evening
sacrifice* (Ezra 9:1-5).

Ezra's solution is starkly clear and uncompromising:

*Therefore do not give your daughters to their sons, neither take their
daughters for your sons, and never seek their peace or prosperity, so
that you may be strong and eat the good of the land and leave it for
an inheritance to your children for ever. ¹³After all that has come
upon us for our evil deeds and for our great guilt, seeing that you,
our God, have punished us less than our iniquities deserved and
have given us such a remnant as this, ¹⁴shall we break your
commandments again and intermarry with the peoples who practice
these abominations? Would you not be angry with us until you
destroy us without remnant or survivor? ¹⁵O LORD, God of
Israel, you are just, but we have escaped as a remnant, as is now
the case. Here we are before you in our guilt, though no one can
face you because of this'* (Ezra 9:12-15).

Not only were future mixed marriages prohibited, but current
marriages were dissolved and all foreign women and wives were
sent away (Ezra 10:19, 44). The just concern to maintain the
covenant was now being manifest in ways that the people were
forgetting that their way of life made it possible for them to be a
light to the nations, not as an excuse for privilege and walling the
people of God off from the nations. Their witness was once again
being forgotten.

The Book of Jonah could have been written by a Jew in
response to fellow Jews, who viewed their calling as a divine status
symbol instead of as their motivation to mission in the world
(though Trible disagrees, "The Book of Jonah," p. 488-489). After
attempting to flee from the task God had given to him to preach
repentance to the people of Nineveh, Jonah fulfilled his task

reluctantly, and when the citizens of that great ancient city repented, Jonah was not happy.

> *But this was very displeasing to Jonah, and he became angry. He prayed to the LORD and said, "O LORD! is not this what I said while I was still in my own country? That is why I fled to Tarshish at the beginning; for I knew that you are a gracious God and merciful, slow to anger, and abounding in steadfast love, and ready to relent from punishing"* (Jonah 4:1-2).

Jonah represents those Israelites who had come to view the nations, the Gentiles, in a disparaging way—as persons worthy only of judgment and destruction. The writer contrasts this view with the very God that Jonah worships as one who is more than ready to forgive and welcome all who repent. The Book of Jonah is a challenge for God's people to be a light to the nations through its witness.

Throughout their history it seemed to be the case that the people of God, Israel, had much difficulty remembering the purpose of their unique character as God's people. Their singular character as God's people, which required Torah obedience, was to be a witness to the world, not a demonstration that they were better than the nations of the world and loved more by God. And they could not be a witness *to* the nations of the world if they acted *like* the nations of the world.

JESUS AND THE RECONSTITUTION OF ISRAEL

The material just surveyed is sketchy and many things have been omitted. The theme of Israel's calling and witness for the sake of the world is not the only narrative thread that runs throughout the Old Testament. But what is critical for our purposes is that it is precisely this storyline that Jesus draws on for his ministry. Just like Jeremiah before him, Jesus will criticize his fellow Jews for failing to be a light to the nations, but first the context must be set in understanding what Jesus was doing when he called his twelve disciples.

That Jesus called twelve disciples was no accident. As Israel consisted of twelve tribes, so Jesus gathered around himself twelve men to take his message of his work to the world. It was a powerful symbolic act in which Jesus was making the extraordinary claim that in his ministry he was reconstituting the people of Israel and its mission of witness to the world. What Jesus was doing was much more than calling a few guys to save souls. He was announcing the revolutionary movement in which God was at last making good on his promise to secure deliverance for Israel and offer that same salvation to the Gentiles as well. The disciples were to be the light to the nations, to bear witness in word and in deed that the God of Israel was going to save the world.

Why did Jesus feel the need to reconstitute Israel in his own ministry? It was because he believed that his own people had failed to do so, and he blamed the religious leaders, the guardians of Israel's covenant.

Then he [Jesus] began to speak to them in parables. 'A man planted a vineyard, put a fence around it, dug a pit for the wine press, and built a watch-tower; then he leased it to tenants and went to another country. ²When the season came, he sent a slave to the tenants to collect from them his share of the produce of the vineyard. ³But they seized him, and beat him, and sent him away empty-handed. ⁴And again he sent another slave to them; this one they beat over the head and insulted. ⁵Then he sent another, and that one they killed. And so it was with many others; some they beat, and others they killed. ⁶He had still one other, a beloved son. Finally he sent him to them, saying, "They will respect my son." ⁷But those tenants said to one another, "This is the heir; come, let us kill him, and the inheritance will be ours." ⁸So they seized him, killed him, and threw him out of the vineyard. ⁹What then will the owner of the vineyard do? He will come and destroy the tenants and give the vineyard to others. ¹⁰Have you not read this scripture:

"The stone that the builders rejected
has become the cornerstone;

¹¹this was the Lord's doing,
and it is amazing in our eyes"?'

¹²When they realized that he had told this parable against them,
they wanted to arrest him, but they feared the crowd. So they left
him and went away (Mark 12:1-12).

For Jesus, one of the biggest failings of his people was the
decision not to reject violence but rather to utilize it as a tool in an
attempt to bring in God's Kingdom. Time and time again, Jesus
continued to insist that God's people could not be a light to the
nations if they insisted on beating the nations over the head. On
more than a few occasions, Jesus refused to be taken off and made
king by the people in order to lead a revolt. For Jesus, the end did
not justify the means; the true end of what God wanted for his
people could not be achieved apart from a certain means. The
world's ways of power and coercion were not to be the ways of
the church. Tom Wright notes, "From [Jesus'] point of view, Israel
at that time was making a pretty poor fist of being the light of the
world. Many of Jesus' contemporaries were hot-headed, zealous
would-be revolutionaries. Was that the way the kingdom would
come? Was that how to be the light of the world?... Jesus' answer
was an unequivocal No (Wright, *The Original Jesus*, p. 49).

Thus, as Jesus seeks to remake the people of God through his
followers, he is clear to them as to how they are to operate among
themselves.

So Jesus called them and said to them, "You know that among the
Gentiles those whom they recognize as their rulers lord it over them,
and their great ones are tyrants over them. ⁴³But it is not so among
you; but whoever wishes to become great among you must be your
servant, ⁴⁴and whoever wishes to be first among you must be slave
of all. ⁴⁵For the Son of Man came not to be served but to serve,
and to give his life a ransom for many" (Mark 10:42-45).

Jesus' words must be understood in their larger context. Jesus
is offering more than a lesson on how the disciples should relate
to one another within the operations of the church community.

Our text also signifies the posture that the followers of Jesus must take as they fulfill the will of God in the world. Mark sets the context for this particular teaching of Jesus:

> *James and John, the sons of Zebedee, came forward to him and said to him, "Teacher, we want you to do for us whatever we ask of you." 36 And he said to them, "What is it you want me to do for you?" 37 And they said to him, "Grant us to sit, one at your right hand and one at your left, in your glory"* (Mark 10:35-37).

James and John are asking Jesus to put them in the two most powerful positions in God's Kingdom—after Jesus, of course. In effect, the two brothers want Jesus to appoint one of them as the Secretary of State and the other as the Secretary of the Treasury. They are thinking of the exercise of power in terms of how all the other nations exercise power. They assume that God's Kingdom will operate accordingly as well. In other words, the Kingdom context of this particular teaching in Mark 10 means that Jesus is not only giving his disciples instructions on how to behave toward one another as they live as God's people, but the posture they are to take toward the world as they bear witness to God's Kingdom.

Jesus, of course, embodies the Kingdom mode of operation throughout his ministry, even refusing to employ the methods of the nations in order to save himself from the horror of the cross. Indeed, Jesus' cross and resurrection revealed the power of the politics of witness over the power politics of the nations. The late John Howard Yoder states, in what has become a classic passage in many Christian circles:

> But the answer given to the question by the series of visions and their hymns [in the Book of Revelation] is not the standard answer. "The lamb that was slain is worthy to receive power!" John is here saying, not as an inscrutable paradox but as a meaningful affirmation, that the cross and not the sword, suffering and not brute power determines the meaning of history. The key to the obedience of God's people is not their effectiveness, but

their patience (13:10). The triumph of the right is assured not by the might that comes to the aid of the right, which is of course the justification of the use of violence and other kinds of power in every human conflict; the triumph of the right, although it is assured, is sure because of the power of the resurrection and not because of any calculation of causes and effects, nor because of the inherently greater strength of the good guys. The relationship between the obedience of God's people and the triumph of God's cause is not a relationship of cause and effect but one of cross and resurrection (John Howard Yoder, *The Politics of Jesus*, p. 238).

So, if this reading of Jesus and his ministry is correct, what has happened to the church is that its political posture in the world seems to look no different from the politics of the nations. Jesus' words of condemnation to the people of Israel seem just as relevant for the church in the twenty-first century West. To make sense of what happened, we need to venture into some church history.

3

The Constantinian Shift:
A (Not So) Funny Thing Happened
on the Way to Rome

By reference to the man Constantine we mean the man less than the period, although the man Constantine did more to consummate the change than any other one person. He certainly was not the only architect of the change. It had begun before him and was not complete until a century after him. It amounted to a fundamental reorientation in the relationship of church and world. – John Howard Yoder

THE CHARACTER OF THE SHIFT

For the first three centuries of its existence the church was a small minority existing in tiny communities all over the mighty Roman Empire. By the time of the fourth century, a decisive shift took place that was in the works for some decades before. In the fourth century the church was still a minority; perhaps three percent of the Empire's population was Christian. But for the first time believers were faced with new questions concerning their relationship to the Empire in which they found themselves.

In order to understand the relationship between church and state and how the politics of witness was supplanted in the church by the politics of power and coercion, we must first set the context of the major shift that took place, which reoriented the way the very character of the church was understood by Christians themselves. The late Mennonite theologian, John Howard Yoder, referred to it as the "Constantinian shift" and for a significant portion of this chapter I will draw from his magisterial work, *Christian Attitudes to War, Peace, and Revolution.*

According to Yoder, the characteristics of this decisive shift were as follows:

First, whereas previously the church did not work hand-in-hand with the empire in furthering the agenda of both, now church and empire worked together. The waves of Roman persecution of Christians failed to stamp out the Christian movement. Emperor Constantine, whose great desire was to unify the empire, decided that the church was the vehicle by which that unity could be secured. Yoder writes, "It was a strategic alliance between two factions in empire politics and it worked. This God helped more than some of the other gods had. Tolerance was proclaimed in 311 and from then on the alliance escalated" (Yoder, *Christian Attitudes*, p. 39).

Second, while the ideal in this new arrangement was that church and empire would assist each other in their mutual endeavors, the empire by far received the best part of the deal. Constantine declares himself the "bishop of bishops" and even presides over the Council of Nicaea in 325 AD. His interest in the Trinitarian controversies was not theological but political. Constantine wanted the church to take the position that would best work toward imperial unity. "Just as other priests of other religions and temples and cults had been under the Caesars, so, now, Christian priests are under the empire and Christian bishops are under the emperor." It was Constantine, said Yoder, who had "the decisive voice" in the decisions of Nicaea even though he had no theological training nor even understood the details of the debate. He was not even baptized until years later in 336 AD, a year before his death (Yoder, *Christian Attitudes*, p. 39).

Third, with this new alliance between church and empire a new ethic had to be forged. Because of the sometimes dirty work of the empire, the church could not expect political officials to live in the same way as other Christians. Since the Christians had no resources to draw on in their frame of reference (they will use the Old Testament) they appealed to pagan sources, the moral philosopher Cicero in particular. Bishop Ambrose and his student, the eventual Bishop Augustine, would work through these sources to develop an ethic for Christians who were officials of the empire. In his usually clear fashion, Yoder gets to the heart of the matter: "In the mind of the churches, this shift is obviously a triumph, but in order to make this victory of the church over the world effective we'll have to use the world's standard for the ethics of Christians in office" (Yoder, *Christian Attitudes*, p. 40).

Fourth, once the empire moves the church from tolerated status, it will not be too long before it becomes favored and in the same position that Roman paganism was in only decades before. Emperor Theodosius (347-395 AD) completes the Constantinian shift. The church is not only officially declared as having the support of the state (at the Council of Constantinople, 381 AD), but pagan temples are closed. Over time it will become a crime not to be a Christian and, in 436 AD, non-Christians are forbidden from military service. Whereas only 300 years before Christians forbade themselves from the army on theological and ecclesiological grounds, they are now the only ones permitted to serve. And while the outward effect of all of this will seem to place great power and influence in the church, what it will in reality do is undermine the church's witness by marginalizing it. The empire will set the agenda for the church to follow.

The Constantinian shift will result in a new understanding of the meaning of history and a radically reshaped ecclesiology, which will have all too real implications for the mission of the church and for the practices of discipleship. Yoder now turns his scholarly gaze toward Eusebius and Augustine and their role in re-forming the church. He writes,

> So you know for a fact that there is a church and that God is using the church for certain ministries of proclamation and service, fellowship, etc. You have to take it on faith that God is governing the world.

> After Constantine, that has fundamentally changed. Eusebius and Augustine, the two great minds of the

fourth and early fifth century, work out an alternative. God is governing history through Constantine. Constantine is not the only person who happened to take the lid off so the Christians could have religious liberty. That is far too little. He is a kind of savior, a kind of bishop, a kind of theologian. The Empire is the church. Therefore the barbarian, the outsider, is now also the infidel, the non-believer. It is fitting that in this visible order of God's work in history there not be liberty for non-Christians or even for dissenting Christians (Yoder, *Christian Attitudes*, pp. 42-43).

With the Constantinian Shift comes a radically new view of the meaning of history. According to the New Testament, God works and moves in history on two levels. Yoder writes, "There is the visible, confessing community, the church. This community celebration is visible. Its confession is open, public. It has a lifestyle different from the neighbors, and the neighbors know it. This voluntary minority body is an organ of the work of God in history" (Yoder, *Christian Attitudes*, p. 42).

On a secondary level, God works invisibly because the risen Christ is now seated at the right hand of the Father. He governs the universe though we are not sure on the specifics. It is impossible to say whether and what happenings in culture and politics have been governed providentially. But the church does affirm that "the risen Lord uses the powers despite themselves, including the economic and political powers, including Caesar, somehow for his political purposes" (Yoder, *Christian Attitudes*, p. 42). Sometimes the church can know what happenings in "secular" history might be the work of God through the prophets or the discernment of the church, but for the most part Christians take it on faith because they know Jesus is Lord.

Visibly there is the church—we know where the church is and how Christians are to live as an alternative to the world as a witness. Invisibly, God is caring for the world. The church is the primary and central vehicle for how God is now working in the world. It is the people of God called to bear witness to the death and resurrection of Jesus in its life and mission to the world. God works elsewhere, but that is clearly secondary.

But after Constantine that has fundamentally changed. God is visibly working through the Empire, working through Constantine. The church comes to believe that whatever happens in reference to the state is the will of God. If Constantine is the emperor, it is because God wants it that way. If Christians are in charge of the Empire, it's because God wants it that way. The possibility of a prophetic witness that claims "God does not want it that way" is muted.

Ecclesiology is now seriously redefined. Yoder states again, "The true church is now invisible. The visible church, obviously, is everybody, because you baptize everybody, except for a few Jews around the edges, who don't count. But you know that most of these baptized are not truly elect in the objective sense.... You know too that most of them are not true believers in the subjective sense, i.e. in the depths of their hearts they are not saved, they are not trusting God for their salvation, they are not loving their neighbors truly" (Yoder, *Christian Attitudes*, p. 43).

So no longer does one look to baptized believers to find the true church—everybody gets baptized who are members of the Empire. Thus the visible church is no longer the primary vehicle by which God moves through history. There is an invisible church, and now you have to take it on faith that God is working though it. But you know for certain that God is working primarily through the state and through the emperor. That is visible. The Empire replaces the church.

Therefore, anyone who truly wants to find the visible church on earth ultimately looks to the bishops and the priests. One will also look to monastic orders and faithful believers who devote their lives to Christ and his church, and who will have to separate themselves off from the world in order to devote themselves to study, prayer, and works of charity. Thus the spiritual disciplines, which should be practiced by every baptized Christian, are now emphasized only among those who are "called" to do so. There certainly will be some regular Christians in the world who will practice such things, but it will no longer be seen as part and parcel of the visible church on earth. Moreover, Augustine and Eusebius will draw their ethics for Christians involved in the business and the affairs of the Empire not from the Bible but from pagan sources. One cannot run an Empire and live according to the Sermon on the Mount, and Caesar will not be expected to do so.

Yoder summarizes the matter well: "[B]efore, you knew as a fact of experience that there was a church, and you had to take it on faith that God was governing history. Now, you know for a fact that God is governing history (Constantine is one of us), but you have to take it on faith that there is a church. That is the shift in the meaning of salvation history for which Constantine is the symbol. That is the philosophical meaning of the Middle Ages, with the eschatology of the New Testament stood on its head" (Yoder, *Christian Attitudes*, p. 44)

IMPLICATIONS OF THE SHIFT

The Constantinian Shift completely reorients the church's identity and mission in the world. Constantine begins a fundamental conversion of the church to the agenda of the empire. The ecclesiological and missional implications are many.

First, the Constantinian Shift undermines the church's distinctiveness as its own nation, its own polis. It is Peter who reminds the early believers that, after the fashion of God's people Israel, they are a royal priesthood, a holy nation (1 Peter 2:9). Now the church no longer views itself as its own entity with its own integrity; it now become the prop, the support for God's nation the Holy Roman Empire. The identity of the church will now be defined by its relationship to the state (so Hauerwas, *In Good Company*, pp. 26-27).

Second, and related to this, is the fact that the Constantinian Shift undermines the church/world distinction. Whereas the church's task previously was to bear witness to the world as to what God wanted the world to be (the church was to be the church) without resorting to the utilization of the power structures of the dominant culture, now the church utilizes those very power structures to fashion a state that favors and even promotes Christianity. Once the empire is viewed as Christian, the church loses its identity as it own nation. Once it becomes illegal for anyone to practice a religion other than Christianity, and once only Christians are allowed to serve in the military with the approval of the church, the primary understanding of God's kingdom as manifest in the state blurs if not completely obliterates the church/world distinction. The Constantinian Shift is complete.

Third, the Constantinian Shift gives divine legitimacy to the state. St. Paul tells the Romans that God desires that there be the order of government and that there is a legitimate place for government to so order society (Romans 13:1-7). But such an understanding of the state is a far cry from the belief that God has called the empire into existence and that God wants this or that particular emperor on the throne. As Yoder reminds us, it is one thing to believe that God uses the empire in spite of itself. It is quite another matter to give the empire divine legitimacy. Romans 13 cannot be correctly understood apart from Romans 12, which begins with a call to nonconformity (Yoder, *The Politics of Jesus*, p.197).

Fourth, the Constantinian Shift undermines Jesus' teaching on the ways of God's Kingdom. I quote again Mark 10:35-45:

> *James and John, the sons of Zebedee, came forward to him and said to him, "Teacher, we want you to do for us whatever we ask of you." And he said to them, "What is it you want me to do for you?" And they said to him, "Grant us to sit, one at your right hand and one at your left, in your glory." But Jesus said to them, "You do not know what you are asking. Are you able to drink the cup that I drink, or be baptized with the baptism that I am baptized with?" They replied, "We are able."*

Then Jesus said to them, "The cup that I drink you will drink; and with the baptism with which I am baptized, you will be baptized; but to sit at my right hand or at my left is not mine to grant, but it is for those for whom it has been prepared."

When the ten heard this, they began to be angry with James and John. So Jesus called them and said to them, "You know that among the Gentiles those whom they recognize as their rulers lord it over them, and their great ones are tyrants over them. But it is not so among you; but whoever wishes to become great among you must be your servant, and whoever wishes to be first among you must be slave of all. For the Son of Man came not to be served but to serve, and to give his life a ransom for many."

Such an upside-down way of operating works as long as the church has no stake in the success of the empire. Once the fortunes of the *ecclesia* are intrinsically bound to the success of the powers, the kingdom ethic of Jesus is marginalized as Christians seek non-Christian sources to inform the ethic of believers as they serve the empire. The kingdom of God comes to earth, not through the mission and witness of the church, but through the political maneuverings and policies of the state. The Sermon on the Mount becomes irrelevant. The cross is no longer relevant as a political model for a church that now has a stake in power of the state. It no longer represents how God would have his people make their way in this world. Indeed, it is by the sign of the cross that Constantine justifies his conquests with the blessing of the church, God's upside-down kingdom that no longer operates as such. The cross no longer represents God's suffering presence in this world through the church but the victorious conquest of the empire in the name of the risen Christ, whose resurrection no longer means the conquest of the powers (Colossians 2:14) but the utilization of the powers to spread the domain of Christ through the empire. In the conversion of Caesar, the church is converted to the ways of the nations. Many centuries later, a group of Enlightenment thinkers will seek to extract the church from the movings and shakings of the state, and in so doing they will ironically reinforce the agenda of the long dead Constantine, an agenda that will continue to reinforce the central importance of the visible empire and the secondary relevance of the invisible church. Thomas Jefferson and Benjamin Franklin will carry out Constantine's centuries old orders as his unwitting but quite effective modern lieutenants.

4
Constantine's Modern Lieutenants: Thomas Jefferson and Benjamin Franklin

Now we start to see why the founding fathers gave so little official favor or protection to Christianity. It was a nice religion to have around for its moral influence, but more central in their minds was not to let it run the country. They had all too much of that back in Europe, with religious wars and partisan excommunications and the rest. They framed a brief amendment that said Congress couldn't "prohibit the free exercise" of religion (so brief a line that we are still arguing in court today, more than two hundred years later, about what the First Amendment really covers and doesn't cover). Beyond that, the churches would just have to make a go of it on their own. – Dean Merrill.

THE NEED FOR THE ENLIGHTENMENT

The Enlightenment was necessary to stop Christians from persecuting and killing each other. Of course, there were other factors that contributed to the rise of the intellectual and philosophical movement that pervaded western Europe and the American colonies in the seventeenth and eighteenth centuries. But the sad and terrible history of Christians persecuting and making war on other Christians played a pivotal role.

It is not possible to survey the major aspects of Enlightenment thinking. There are plenty of good surveys available. But what is important to note is that many Enlightenment thinkers rejected many traditional doctrines of Christianity for two reasons. First, they believed that many of those doctrines could not stand up to the test of reason, and second, it was precisely the disagreement over those doctrines that led to persecutions and inquisitions and violence. Catholics persecuted the Protestant Reformers for their belief that the Bible should be made available to the common folks, then the Reformers turned around and killed the Anabaptists for the rejection of infant baptism. Meanwhile, in seventeenth century England, Protestants and Catholics suffered violence at the hands of each other depending on the faith embraced by the current monarch on the throne. Is it any wonder that doctrine left a bad taste in the mouths of many?

In allowing for the free exercise of religion but not recognizing religion as a state sponsored entity, two things happened that are of concern to us in this chapter: (1) religion was marginalized in various capacities from the seat of governmental power, and yet (2) religion became a tool of the state when necessary to achieve its desired ends. While many Enlightenment thinkers contributed to the subject of our concern in this chapter, the two who stand out are Thomas Jefferson and Benjamin Franklin.

JEFFERSON

Of all the Founders, no one placed his philosophical mark on the new nation of the United States more than Thomas Jefferson (James Madison was a close second). Jefferson was truly a son of the Enlightenment, embracing deism and rejecting traditional expressions of Christianity without reservation.

Like most deists, Jefferson did not believe that God was intimately involved in human affairs, and Christian doctrines that explicitly stated so, like the Incarnation, the authority of Scripture, and the resurrection of Jesus, were to be rejected as the "deliria of crazy imaginations." Jefferson referred to the doctrine of the Trinity as "mere abracadabra" (Merrill, *Sinners in the Hands of an Angry Church*, p. 89). Jefferson did, however, believe that individuals would be judged by God for their deeds, though the idea of any kind of eternal state of damnation was anathema (Sanford, *The Religious Life of Thomas Jefferson*, p. 145). For Jefferson, like other deists, the chief contribution of religion was to make moral people and good citizens. Doctrine was irrelevant. Jefferson did suggest, however, that on rare occasions God might answer prayer.

Jefferson did not have a very high view of the clergy as a profession. Throughout his life he referred to all clergy, including Protestant pastors, as "priests." The term, in his context, was not a compliment. Jefferson believed that priests, like kings, were enemies of individual freedom, and that such doctrines as the Trinity were simply used by the clergy to retain their manipulative power over the people. In a letter to John Adams, Jefferson wrote, "It is too late in the day for men of sincerity to pretend they believe in the Platonic mysticisms that three are one, and one is three; and yet that the one is not three, and the three are not one.... But this constitutes the craft, power, and the profit of the priests" (Mapp, *The Faiths of Our Fathers*, p.11). Jefferson believed that the power the clergy exercised historically in Europe and the colonies was enough of an argument to exclude them from holding public office. It must be said, however, that while Jefferson was distrustful of the clergy as an institution (especially Catholic priests—Jefferson had little good to say about Catholicism), he did speak well of individual "priests" who did much charitable good in the community, and he was good friends with a liberal minister and scientist, Joseph Priestly. (The irony of Priestly's last name should not be missed.)

Jefferson loved what he called the good and simple religion of Jesus. His problem was not with Jesus but with how, so he believed, his followers distorted his teaching. The two Christian figures Jefferson reserved his harshest literary venom for were St. Paul and John Calvin. For Jefferson, Paul turned Jesus, the great moral deistic teacher (Jefferson actually referred to Jesus as a deist), into a divine Savior who redeemed the world in slaughterhouse fashion for a blood-thirsty deity. Calvin added to Paul's distortion of Jesus with his doctrine of original sin, which erroneously claimed humanity's helplessness before God, and double-predestination in which God decided by fiat who was to be saved and who was to be damned. Jefferson found all of this to be absurd.

Jefferson's most well known views on religion were his thoughts he offered on the Bible itself. Jefferson embraced the teaching of Jesus as simple enough to be understood by a child, but rejected what he could not stomach (his words) as the unreasonable parts of Scripture, particularly the Gospels' stories of miracles including the resurrection. Near the end of his life, though it was a project started years before while he was president, Jefferson took scissors to the Gospels and cut out the parts of the four Gospels he believed to be the authentic teachings of Jesus and arranged them into a narrative of the "most pure, benevolent, and sublime [teachings] which have ever been preached to man." He did not allow the work to be published during his lifetime. (It was published after his death.) The final work, which came to be known as *The Jefferson Bible*, is still in print to this day.

Jefferson was extremely concerned with the practice or ritual of government, which undermined his exclusionary understanding of the separation of church and state. Both Presidents Washington and Adams had proclaimed national days of prayer, fasting, and thanksgivings. Jefferson stopped the practice during his administration because he said it was "too Christian a thing for the president to do."

Toward the end of his life, Jefferson started to speak of God in more personal terms. While he continued to use the preferred deistic language of Providence and Creator, he began to refer to the deity as "God" and even "my God." In his old age attending worship (Jefferson was always fairly active in church attendance), witnesses noted that Jefferson frequently teared up as the old hymns were sung. It would be foolish to conclude from this that Jefferson began to embrace the doctrines expressed in those hymns that deists considered to be outdated, since there is nothing in his later writings that remotely hint at such a thing. Rather, the tears were more likely the sentimental reminiscing of an old man who remembered singing those same hymns as a young boy with his sister by the light of the evening fire.

FRANKLIN

Benjamin Franklin was born in Boston, Massachusetts in 1706 and raised in a Puritan home in which his father Josiah taught a strict Calvinism of election and reprobation. Franklin would come to reject both as a young and inquisitive man in his teens. He would consider atheism as a logical possibility (in his early years he often used the terms "deism" and "atheism" interchangeably). Franklin would not consider atheism for very long, but he would never return to his Puritan Calvinist roots. He would instead embrace deism, finding that the arguments in its favor were more convincing than those against.

In his younger years Franklin held to the odd belief that all persons received an equal share of pleasure and suffering in life, but changed his opinion because of his conviction that King George III was the worst international villain of the eighteenth century (which was not true) and the source of terrible suffering for the colonists.

Franklin believed that it was important to spread the teachings of Jesus but seriously doubted his divinity. Indeed, Franklin believed that promoting the teachings of Socrates was be just as important as those of Jesus. Unlike some other Founders who were semi-regular to regular church goers, Franklin showed very little interest in attending public worship. He did enjoy the sermons of George Whitefield, but found too much preaching to be centered on dogma and doctrine, and not virtue. Upon listening to a Presbyterian pastor for five consecutive weeks, Franklin complained that his aim was "rather to make us good Presbyterians than good citizens" (Issacson, *Benjamin Franklin*, p. 84). Indeed, Franklin believed that the church's main purpose was to make good citizens.

It was virtue that concerned Franklin the most in reference to religion and citizenship. Like Franklin, the major Founders emphasized the ethical implications of religion. What was important was not doctrinal speculation but what kind of citizens religion produced. But no Founder comes close to Franklin in reference to working out virtue and morality in his writings. He expressed such a strong belief in how one lived over what one believed that, in a letter to his brother John, he stated, "I should have more dependence on works than on faith" (Isaacson, *Benjamin Franklin*, p. 87).

To that end, Franklin's religion was very pragmatic. He expressed serious doubts that God answers prayer, though he thought prayer acceptable because it certainly couldn't hurt. He was, however, opposed to prayer as a justification for human inaction. His pragmatism led him to embark on a revision of the Book of Common Prayer, modernizing the language and shortening its redundancies. He also suggested that the churches should shorten their services because the infirm could not tolerate being in a cold and damp environment for so long and because shorter worship might attract younger people. This religious pragmatism was evident in Franklin even at a young age, when he suggested to his father that offering grace over the meat while it was still in the barrel would save time instead of saying it over just a portion at every meal. During a tense moment at the Constitutional Convention of 1787, Franklin suggested that the proceedings pause for a time of prayer. Considering Franklin's views on prayer, what he suggested was probably less about prayer and more a pragmatic way of introducing some serenity into the Convention. It didn't work—the Convention debated Franklin's suggestion for twenty minutes before deciding against it.

In his younger years Franklin expressed doubt about an afterlife, but in his later years he expressed the doctrine more in terms of hope than of doubt. His hope was not based on the Bible, but on his observations of nature, which Franklin called the "Book of Nature," a book to be read as a primary text for Devotees of Reason.

At the age of twenty-two, Benjamin Franklin wrote the following for his epitaph, which was not engraved on his tombstone:

The body of Benjamin Franklin, Printer (like the cover of an old book; its contents torn out and stripped of its lettering and gilding), lies here, food for worms; but the work shall not be lost, for it will (as he believed) appear once more in a new and more elegant edition, revised and corrected by the Author.

Franklin's views on immortality were clearly informed by his observations of nature. Franklin never mentions Jesus' resurrection when discussing the topic.

CONSTANTINE'S MODERN LIEUTENANTS?

It should be beyond dispute that both Thomas Jefferson and Benjamin Franklin did not favor a strong and influential role of the church in the politics of statecraft. But it isn't a stretch to suggest that they in effect carried out Constantine's agenda many centuries later. It was Constantine who wanted an alliance with the church to achieve his own political ends. Jefferson and Franklin wanted the precepts of religion out of the halls of state power, but wanted its moral influence to further the political ends of the state.

It is true that Enlightenment thinkers, like Jefferson and Franklin, were opposed to a coalition between church and state, but that is why I refer to both men as Constantine's *unwitting* modern lieutenants. While they never would have supported a state favored or sponsored religion the way Constantine did, their understanding of doctrine as irrelevant for public discourse and their reductionist perspective on religion as embodying tame virtue in effect continued the same agenda of the domestication of the church in order to do the bidding of the state.

By marginalizing Christian doctrine to the realm of nothing more than private reflections having nothing to do with public reality, they were essentially attempting to strip Christianity of its unique identity. Doctrine is, in one sense, the intellectual substance of Christianity. Jefferson may have believed that the doctrine of the Trinity was "mere abracadabra," but the Gospel of John employs the relationship between the Father and the Son as a model for unity among believers (John 17:20-21). Franklin may have thought that the belief in Jesus' resurrection was irrelevant to the afterlife, but St. Paul seemed to think that not only did the Christian faith rest on its truth (1 Corinthians 15:16-19), but that the resurrection of Christ was essentially instrumental for Christian virtue and living (Colossians 3). The modern Western attempt to privatize doctrine was also an effort to take away the distinctive of Christian identity. Once this happens, accounts of virtue are no longer intelligible as Christian; indeed it is even worse than that—accounts of "Christian" virtue become nothing more than explications of civic virtue. Benjamin Franklin thus gets his way: the task of that Presbyterian pastor Franklin listened to was not to make good Presbyterians in his preaching, but good citizens that would be loyal to the state.

Of course, once Christian identity is gutted of its public witness (because its doctrine has become nothing more than a matter of personal preference), the church by necessity will identify with the culture that now surrounds it and the state powers that rule over it. If nature abhors a vacuum, then virtue cannot tolerate amnesia. The Jefferson Bible becomes the epitome of the Enlightenment's attempt to remake Christianity by cutting out its central core and substituting something else—an account of Jesus that reduces him to a good moral teacher who inhabited the best of Enlightenment deism and morality. Thus the church is marginalized to the edge of relevance in the halls of power, but it is still necessary for instilling in the American citizenry the ethics of Jesus, which is now nothing more than a thin veneer for civic virtue.

The irony here simply cannot be missed. Jefferson and Franklin reject a Constantinianism that forged too close of an alliance between the empire and the church, but their account of church and state and religion simply reinforce in practice the results of Constantinianism (and Christendom) by marginalizing the church from the power of statecraft while manipulating and using the church for its own purposes—training its flocks not to be virtuous Christians in the vision of the New Testament, but to be virtuous people that will be virtuous citizens on behalf of the state. If it is true that Constantinianism was the church's attempt to be politically relevant, the same is true with the church's acceptance of its role as the modern state's virtue processing plant; and the result of both projects remains the same—in the name of being politically relevant, the church becomes politically invisible (see Hauerwas, *Hannah's Child*, p. 160). Christians have been duped into believing that political relevance can only be had by participation in the inner workings of statecraft. We have come to believe that lie because our unique identity as the body of Christ, God's nation in this world, has been seriously compromised. Hauerwas and Willimon state,

> ...we are told that we must deal with the perennial question of the relationship between Christ and culture. The problem with putting the issue that way is that it presumes that the church, and the Christ we worship, is not itself a culture. The problem before us today is not how the church will serve its culture. We are already servile to this culture in too many ways!
>
> The question is, How can the church be enculturated as a people capable of surviving in a culture that tempts us to forget that we ourselves, as the church, are a culture? How can our culture be an alternative to the cultures in which we find ourselves? Of course, there may be continuities between the culture that is the church and the culture in which we find ourselves. Cultural continuity, however, cannot be guaranteed, or desired, for much depends on how open a surrounding culture is to those who worship God. This continuity is something that the church discovers because it first knows who it is (Hauerwas and Willimon, *Where Resident Aliens Live*, p. 39).

Both Constantinianism and Enlightenment rationalism view politics as centrally located in the nation state. The problem has been that, since the fourth century, most Christians have believed the same. Indeed, Christians have been largely responsible in building both! Because we have largely forgotten that the church is its own nation and its own culture and its own polity, we have undermined our mission as the church and have failed to realize that the primary way in which we are political in this world is through our witness. The church allowed Constantine to frame the reality. Jefferson and Franklin and their compatriots simply reinforced that reality.

While Thomas Jefferson's Bible was his attempt to remake the Christianity of the Bible, several orthodox Christians were assisting him in their own biblical reinterpretations of texts, especially those passages that refer specifically to and were meant decisively for Israel and the Church. They may not have flatly denied the essential doctrines of the faith, but they aided and abetted Jefferson in undermining the singular significance of these two communities of faith that produced the Scriptures and were nourished by them at the well of God's wisdom.

5

It's Israel and the Church, Not Israel and America: An Ecclesial Hermeneutic

We currently have difficulty in appreciating the moral role of scripture because we have forgotten that the authority of scripture is a political claim characteristic of a very particular kind of polity. By "political" I do not mean, as many who identify with liberation theology, that scripture should be used as an ideology for justifying the demands of the oppressed. The authority of scripture derives its intelligibility from the existence of a community that knows its life depends on faithful remembering of God's care of his creation through the calling of Israel and the life of Jesus. — Stanley Hauerwas.

THE MIRROR HERMENEUTICS OF THE RELIGIOUS RIGHT AND THE RELIGIOUS LEFT

I begin this chapter by appealing to the argument of James Hunter in his book, *To Change the World*. Hunter persuasively argues that the religious right and the religious left are nothing more than mirror images of each other (see also Bevere, *All Is Not As It Seems*, pp. 49-53). The civil religion of the religious right should be obvious to everyone paying even superficial attention to religion and politics in America. But, as Hunter points out, the religious left has a civil religion that is basically the same in character as Christians on the other side of the political aisle, *and both groups are centered on a faulty hermeneutic (method of biblical interpretation)*. In this chapter we will focus primarily on the religious left. Whereas the religious right has undergone intense scrutiny over its promotion of civil religion over the past few years, the civil religion of the left has been virtually ignored. Part of the reason is that many on the religious right publicly embrace civil religion, while those on the religious left continue to deny the truth about their politics and their own brand of civil religion that they obviously support.

Hunter defines civil religion as "a diffuse amalgamation of religious values that is synthesized with the civic creeds of the nation; in which the life and mission of the church is conflated with the life and mission of the country. American values are, in substance, biblical prophetic values; American identity is, thus, vaguely Christian identity" (Hunter, *To Change the World*, p. 145).

The religious right has used Scripture for years to commend to the state what its positions on domestic and foreign policy should be. Romans 1 and the Old Testament Book of Leviticus are employed to oppose gay marriage. 2 Corinthians 9:7 is quoted to oppose government taxation for social programs. And 2 Chronicles 7:14 is used as the rallying cry for a "national revival."

"If my people, who are called by my name will humble themselves and pray..." is interpreted as referring to the people of America. The problem, however, is that God is speaking to his people Israel. No modern nation can rightfully claim to be the people of God. The Bible reserves the language of divine peoplehood for two "nations" alone—Israel and the Church. Thus, when Christians interpret that verse in reference to the United States, they misinterpret it. If 2 Chronicles 7:14 is to be a rallying cry for revival in the twenty-first century, it should be directed at the people of God, the church.

But the religious left is no different. It may be that Christians on the left in some places are more uncomfortable with patriotic worship services in church than the religious right, which seems to relish such moments. As Hunter rightly observes, "Jim Wallis, among other politically progressive Christians, has rightly complained that the Christian Right is engaged in promoting 'civil religion' rather than in biblical Christianity.... Yet Wallis and others in the Evangelical Left engage in the identical practice for which they criticize the Christian Right" (Hunter, *To Change the World*, p. 145).

Moreover, like the religious right, the religious left utilizes the biblical values of Scripture to commend to the state what its policies should be on various issues. The following is a partial list from Hunter:

√ Government budgets and tax policies should show compassion for the poor and foreign policy should include such considerations as fair trade (Matthew 2:34-40, Isaiah 10:1-2)
√ Government officials should tell the truth in what is truly going on in foreign and domestic policies (John 8:32)
√ Policies on abortion, capital punishment, euthanasia, HIV/AIDS, and genocide (to name a few) should follow the biblical injunction to choose life (Deuteronomy 30:19)
√ "Wallis even quotes Isaiah in defense of an increase in the minimum wage" (Hunter, To Change the World, p.147).

The issue here is not that truth telling is a bad idea or that care for the poor is of no concern or that the unborn should not be protected. The dilemma again is a hermeneutical one. Hunter's conclusion is spot on:

> The problem, of course, is that Amos, Micah, Isaiah, and the other prophets were living in a Jewish theocratic setting. The only way that Wallis and others can make these strong statements is to confuse America with Israel and the political dynamics of modern American democracy with the divine laws mandated for ancient Israel. It isn't that the wisdom of scripture is irrelevant for the formation of political values, but one can only make the close associations and specific political judgments Wallis does by turning progressive religion into a civil religion of the Left.... Both Right and Left, then, aspire to a righteous empire. Thus, when he [Wallis] accuses Falwell and Robertson of being "theocrats who desire their religious agenda to be enforced through the

power of the state" he has established the criteria by which he and other politically progressive Christians are judged the same (Hunter, *To Change the World*, p.147).

If the religious right and the left want to get the target of their hermeneutic correct, they need to understand that the commands of Scripture in the Old Testament are, by and large, directed toward the people of God Israel, and that the New Testament writers shift that focus to God's people the church, while not rejecting that they still apply to Israel. It is the people of God that is to embody the prophets' concern for justice and the Torah's concern for morality and purity. And it is by that biblically based way of life that the church engages in the politics of witness that it is God and not the nations who rules the world. The church by its example bears witness to the nations as to what God wants of them as well. The church by its witness is not a prop for the state, but its alternative.

IT'S ISRAEL AND THE CHURCH

Once the nation becomes the primary hermeneutical target of Scripture, the primary community of faith becomes the state. The church is eclipsed in this world and so is the kingdom of God.

And once the state becomes the primary community of faith because the Scriptures are applied primarily to the state, civil religion is at hand. The church no longer plays the role of prophet to the nation; it becomes a puppet of the state.

This is not to deny that God will hold the nations accountable or that there are some harsh words from God to them (Amos 1:2-2:3). But when admonitions, which are clearly directed to God's people, are interpreted primarily as referring to the nations, one cannot avoid the conclusion that such a hermeneutic assumes the nation state to be primarily God's people, while the true people of God, the church, are left as nothing more than cheerleaders to support the state's agenda with the goal of being power-brokers on Pennsylvania Avenue and Capitol Hill.

Thus the hermeneutical posture the church must take is to understand that the admonitions of the prophets and the Sermon on the Mount (just two examples) are directed to the people of God, and we the church must embody in our corporate worship and service as well as in our individual discipleship lives that witness to the nations what God wants. In other words, the church's first task is not to work to coerce the state to take care of the poor. The church's first task is to live lives of simplicity and generosity and take care of the poor ourselves. In so doing we will be witnessing to the nation that it would be a better state if it took care of the poor as well. The church's first task is not to coerce the state into outlawing abortions. The church's first task is to reject abortion as a Christian option and live in such a way that we welcome all children into the world. In so doing we will be witnessing to the nation (as Tertullian stated to the Roman Empire) that it would be a better state if it didn't kill its children. Unfortunately, such an approach to social issues is problematic for most Christians because they have come to believe that the law is much more than simply a modest helper (Merrill, *Sinners in the Hands of an Angry Church*, p. 34). They have embraced legislation as the central focus of societal change.

"If my people, which are called by my name" (2 Chronicles 7:14) should not be read in church on the Fourth of July; it should be read instead on Ash Wednesday. "He has told you, O mortal, what is good; and what does the LORD require of you but to do justice, and to love kindness, and to walk humbly with your God?" (Micah 6:8) should not be employed when Christians argue over who to vote for; it should be called upon to remind Christians of how their materialism leads to injustice for others.

If God's people can embody Scripture in their lives and avoid the faulty hermeneutic that marginalizes the church as the center of God's politics with the state, then we can recover the politics of witness to the powers that surround us. But the politics of witness can only be recovered with a renewed and robust political ecclesiology and a hermeneutic that does justice to the place of the church in the world.

6
Why the Church in America
Cannot Speak Truth to Power

Political Activism carries unique dangers for the church while offering real, but limited, kingdom opportunities. The danger is to become too close to a particular political ideology and to accommodate Jesus' call to discipleship to a worldly power strategy or power center. — Glen Stassen and David Gushee.

THE POWER PROBLEM

This chapter begins like the last one did—with James Hunter, who also turns his critical gaze toward the religious right and the religious left and their employment of power politics. Hunter rightly concludes that they are close relatives who dislike each other and yet think they are not related. Such is the mythology perpetrated on both sides. As Hunter cogently argues, both the right and the left seek political power in order to fundamentally transform America according to their understanding of biblical values while ending up being nothing more than faith-based extensions of the Republican and Democratic Parties.

Hunter understands that power is exercised in more than one way and that ultimately it is impossible not to resort to power of some kind. To use one's influence on someone else is to resort to power. But what Hunter argues is that the problem with both the religious right and the religious left is that they "operate with an understanding of power that is derived from the larger and dominant culture of the late modern world" (Hunter, *To Change the World*, p. 100). The implication of this is clear—both sides derive their understanding of power politics more from modern displays of the rough and tumble of modern politics than from the New Testament.

The power motivation among the populists of the Christian right is the adherence to the mythology that America was founded as a Christian nation. Since the nation's founders were Christians they incorporated Christian principles into the nation's foundational political documents. America from the beginning was Christian. To turn the United States into a secular state would be to erode its foundations, not bolster them.

Those Christian conservatives who are knowledgeable in the area of American history and religion rightly reject the clear and direct claim that America is a Christian nation (see Beckwith, *Politics for Christians*, pp. 33-35; Boyd, *The Myth of a Christian Nation*, pp. 12-15). Their power motivation is based on a more nuanced understanding of the place of religion in the early years of America. These members of the religious right argue that "faith (both Jewish and Christian) was an active part of its history. Not only was it a personal reality of the majority of people, it also provided the motivation for public service, the language of public discourse, and the terms for the long pursuit of public justice" (Hunter, *To Change the World*, p. 113).

However, even though the latter group of Christian conservatives have a more serious and believable account of religion in the public political arena, they still resort to the same modern modes of power politics because "America belongs to people of faith.... it was their faith that provided the spiritual and moral foundations for America's greatness" (Hunter, *To Change the World*, pp. 114, 115).

If the power motivation of the religious right is to keep America a Christian nation, the power motivation of the religious left is to make America Christian. Of course, those on the left protest immediately that this is not their agenda, but the evidence clearly demonstrates otherwise. As was suggested in the last chapter, the emphasis on justice in particular as it is interpreted from the Old Testament prophets and in the teaching of Jesus is how the religious left seeks to reshape America after this biblical image. Both mainline liberals and evangelical progressives have this power motivation in common. Hunter notes that some on the religious left forget the influence of mainline Protestantism on politics in the early and middle parts of the twentieth century. Hunter notes, "Politically progressive Christianity achieved its apex of visibility and influence in the middle decades of the twentieth century. Most of the major mainline denominations had their social justice ministries that lobbied on behalf of particular public policy in Washington D.C., as of course did such ecumenical bodies as the National Council of Churches" (Hunter, *To Change the World*, p. 134).

Evangelical progressives have now picked up the mainline progressive power agenda. In particular, Hunter turns his critical gaze toward "the most visible figure of this movement," Jim Wallis. It has been the resurgence of the evangelical left in recent years that led Wallis to proclaim that "the monologue of the religious right is over; a new dialogue has begun." But as Hunter notes, it was the liberals in the mainline churches that owned the original political monologue.

Unlike the religious right, which is honest and direct about wanting America to reflect Christian values, the religious left denies that such is their agenda. Their actual words, however, betray their denials. In his book, *God's Politics*, Wallis utilizes Scripture (as we saw in the last chapter) to commend what government should do, including referencing Micah 4:1-4 "as the standard for American foreign policy" and Isaiah 65:20-25 as "the standard by which to measure the Federal budget" (146). (Can one imagine how Wallis would have reacted had the late Jerry Falwell published a book entitled, *God's Politics*?)

Hunter refers to Katha Pollitt, who writes in *The Nation* (a politically progressive opinion journal) that Wallis is just as much a power player as Pat Robertson. In Pollitt's own words, "by a remarkable act of providence, God's politics turns out to be curiously tailored to the current crisis of the Democratic Party."

Hunter concludes with words that apply both to the religious right and the left their "ideal is to spawn a movement that will create an irresistible 'change in the wind.' The framework by which change is enacted, however, is the State—its rituals, practices, laws, policies, and procedures" (Hunter, *To Change the World*, p. 145).

Thus, while the power motivations of the religious left and the religious right are somewhat different though related, both ultimately have the same agenda—"control over the power of the State" (149). Both sides seek to remake America after their own Christian vision. The kingdom of God comes to earth, not through the mission and witness of the church, but through the political maneuverings of Capitol Hill and Pennsylvania Avenue. The Sermon on the Mount becomes irrelevant. Vernard Eller drives the point home:

> I am convinced that there are many Christians (of both the left and right) who, as individuals, are quite modest, humble, and of realistic self-image—but, who then, proceed to satisfy their lust for power, their delusions of grandeur, and their sense of self-righteousness through the holy archys with which they identify. Asserting their "just cause" becomes a psychological disguise for asserting themselves; thus they find Christian justification for the sense of power to which all of us are tempted (Eller, *Christian Anarchy*, p. 27; quoted in Black, *Christian Archy*, pp. 6-7).

Indeed, as we saw in the previous chapter in reference to hermeneutics, the entirety of the religious right and the religious left are simply two sides of the same modern political coin.

THE CHURCH IS NOT NATHAN AND WASHINGTON D.C. IS NOT KING DAVID

There are many political catch-phrases that have become useless in modern politics—phrases like "the politics of fear," "the politicizing of whatever," "the culture of corruption." The reason such phraseology is useless is because both sides of the political aisle insist that only the other side engages in such tactics. Thus such phraseology is vacuous. But perhaps the most useless political phrase of all is the high-sounding but irrelevant phraseology of "speaking truth to power."

Many years ago, philosopher Alasdair McIntyre wrote the wonderful book, *Whose Justice, Which Rationality,* in which he argued that all conceptions of justice and rationality presuppose a tradition that give them definition. Likewise, the notions of "truth" and "power" are not universal terms that everyone understands; rather they too presuppose a tradition, a context, a narrative that make them intelligible.

So, why is it that the church in America today cannot speak truth to power? Let me synthesize the first section of this chapter while adding some additional thoughts.

The reasons are two-fold: First, the vast majority of Christians in America have accepted the Constantinian notion that the primary political task of the church is to rule, to be in charge. What that means at the very least is that Christians are to play a prophetic role in the political court of Washington D.C. Second, it means that most Christians have accepted the modern dichotomies (and false dichotomies in biblical terms) of left/right, liberal/conservative, Democrat/Republican.

In accepting these two "truths," the problem becomes clear. As Christians, instead of identifying ourselves as primarily kingdom citizens, we see ourselves first and foremost as Democrats or Republicans, conservatives or liberals. The Sermon on the Mount gets eclipsed by the political platforms of the DNC and the RNC. We like to say that we transcend such earthly contrived political conventions, but we can point to very little evidence to show that this is indeed the case. James Dobson is clearly a conservative Republican and Jim Wallis is obviously a liberal Democrat. The only truth they speak to power is their own Republican or Democratic truth to the power of the other party. Criticism of their own is basically absent or woefully inadequate at best. It appears that both men desire to play the role of Nathan in David's court, but they find they only have influence in that court when "David" is part of their own party, and then their prophetic denunciations are reserved only for the opposition outside the court and not those who are in power. They have very little of a prophetic nature to say to the king from their own party whom they serve. In other words, the church cannot speak truth to power because the church itself is up to its armpits in the power of the state and, therefore, has a stake in such power.

In cozying up to the principalities and powers, Christians on the left and the right have chosen the politics of power over the politics of witness; indeed, they cannot even imagine, in spite of what they say, what the politics of the Kingdom of God might look like apart from the politics of left and right. Take the recent health care debate as an example. Christians on the left argue that health care is a right, and Christians on the right argue that health care is a commodity—and neither side bothers to consider the possibility that both "rights" and "commodities" are notions not found in Scripture or that both concepts are theologically problematic.

In accepting the above named two-fold presuppositions, Christians speak the same language as everyone else, thus making it far from clear why Christianity even matters in the public sphere. And suggesting that what makes an argument Christian is that it shows concern for the poor and the outcast does not make an argument specifically Christian. For Christians to be concerned for the poor, the outcasts, and those on the fringes of society should be a given. The problem is that it is not always clear how Christians should care for such persons. Christians are oriented in theology and ethics not in their concern for the poor, but in how the world has now been changed and redefined in the cross and resurrection of Jesus Christ.

And therein lies the heart of the problem. That most Christians in America believe that the church's primary role is to affect policy in Washington D.C. betrays the mistaken belief that the primary political action in this world is to be found in the White House and on Capitol Hill, when the New Testament clearly indicates that the primary agency of politics is located in nothing less than the community of faith known as the church. In order for the church to speak truth to power it must recover its unique polity apart from the earthly polity known as the nation state, for it is God, and not the nations, who rules the world.

My great concern is that when Christians in America want to play the role of prophet in Pharaoh's court, they end up looking, not like the wise sage, but the court jester that gets used by the king for his or her own comical and unsavory purposes.

It should be clear by now that something is amiss when it comes to the church and politics. It seems as if the ghost of the Emperor Constantine is still with us. It appears as if both the religious right and the religious left assume that the political task of Christians is to rule, to be in charge, and that the responsibility of Christians is to work to elect faithful (meaning left-leaning or right-leaning candidates depending on one's politics) Christians (or non-Christians who share certain views deemed as Christian) to the Oval Office and the halls of Congress. I question how all of this squares with the cross of Christ.

Let me be clear: it is not a question of whether or not the church should be political; Jesus was crucified for treason with good reason. It is not a question of *whether*, but of *how* the church should be political. And while both the religious right and the religious left help us think through the "how," I am doubtful that ultimately they are helpful, because what they are about is too wrapped up in the politics of the nation state that is passing away. The more I work through this, the more I am coming to believe that the church should marginalize its agenda of control and recover once again the central significance of the politics of witness. It is God and not the nations who rules the world; it is the church that is the most significant polity in human history, as it uniquely bears witness to the Lordship of Jesus Christ.

What I have been suggesting throughout this book is that the people of God have been co-opted by the state. It is therefore time for the church to recover the politics of witness—of being the nation God intends for us to be by embodying in our ecclesial life the politics of the Kingdom of God, and thereby witnessing to the world what God desires of it as well.

7
The Politics of Witness:
A (Not So) Modest Proposal

Christendom is an effort of the human race to go back to walking on all fours, to get rid of Christianity, to do it knavishly under the pretext that this is Christianity, claiming that it is Christianity perfected. The Christianity of Christendom transforms Christianity into something entirely different from what is in the New Testament, yea, into exactly the opposite. — Søren Kierkegaard.

"So, I think I understand what you are saying, but how does this look?" That's a question I get frequently from people. They do not necessarily take issue with me on the basics of my account but are unsure of what a church would look like that embodied this robust political ecclesiology of witness. It's a fair question and a good one. Before I attempt my (not so) modest proposal, let me clarify what the politics of witness does not mean and suggest why I believe so many Christians have trouble wrapping their minds around this vision of the church and politics.

THE POLITICS OF WITNESS IS NOT...

First, the politics of witness does not promote withdrawal from the world. That's usually the misinterpretation of my position. Indeed, the politics of witness promotes an even more robust engagement with the world. Instead of looking first and foremost to forge an alliance with the government, the politics of witness insists that the church embody in its mission what God wants of it in order to be the light of the world Jesus wants it to be (Matthew 5:14-16). Scot McKnight puts it well:

Instead of American and Western Christians anchoring their hope in the political process, instead of waging war in the public forum for platform issues, and instead of the ups and downs of hope and despair that arise in the election process, I contend the Politics of Jesus is the Church and, in particular, your local church.

Jesus' politics is a body of people living an alternative life. Jesus' politics is kingdom living in the here and now. Jesus' politics are not concerned with power, but the revolutionary power of love and service and justice and peace and wisdom. Jesus' politics is nothing short of the power of kingdom holiness.

In the Politics of Jesus, we find an imagination fired by parabolic visions of a different order. We find an eschatology anchored in the act of God through his people. We find a power that emerges from the Holy Spirit. We find a community with a mission to serve its community instead of being served by that community.

Instead of exploitation, we find extension. Instead of violence, we find peace. Instead of acquisition, we find giving (McKnight, "Converting Our Imagination 6").

Second, the politics of witness is not apolitical. That should be obvious by the phrase "the *politics* of witness." The issue is not whether or not the church will be political; it is a matter of how it will be political. As I have already stated a few times, the politics of witness proceeds on the assumption that the church is where the true political action is and not the nation state.

Third, the politics of witness is not a complete rejection of the nation state and the possibility that it may and must seek the common good; but it a highly qualified possibility. The Bible certainly indicates that God expects the nations to act justly and that he will hold them accountable for doing so (cf. Isaiah 10:1-19). The politics of witness does not preclude the church working with the nation on matters that benefit the common good, but that is *not* the primary political task of the church. Its principal political charge is to show the nations in its mission what God expects of them. When the politics of the church is first and foremost viewed as forging alliances with the state and playing power politics in the halls of government, the message of the gospel and the mission of the church are undermined. Indeed, when such alliances are forged and power games are played by Christians who have come to believe that the political action is in Washington D.C., America becomes the church for such Christians on the religious right and the religious left. As Douglas Harink notes,

> All discourse about God, faith, and the church is so thoroughly co-opted into the project of making America a better nation, that it is never allowed to *fundamentally disrupt* the solipsistic discourse of the American social and political project. In other words, there is something *fundamentally idolatrous* about Wallis's theological discourse; it is certainly no less idolatrous than the discourse of the Religious Right which Wallis is very good at exposing. Unless Christian discourse about God, faith and the church is allowed in the first place to be absolutely free of its *usefulness* for Americanism, it will always be idolatrous.

> The good news of the Gospel of Jesus Christ is that it is God's radical and decisive invasion of our humanly constructed worlds, and God's deliverance from and destruction of the powers that hold us in bondage. The American nation, or the Canadian nation, or any other nation for that matter, is a *humanly constructed world*; it is *a power that enslaves human beings* and makes us serve its ends. Every nation is in the first place an idolatrous regime to which God comes in the Gospel to set his people free. Before the *church* and its discourse can be of any use to American people, it must learn that it does not exist in the first place as America, or to be of use to America, but it exists as the church, constituted in its worship and

service of the one true God (Harink, "God's Politics?").

Scot McKnight adds his wisdom to the matter as well:

> Christians become idolatrous when they believe more in
> the State than the Church (not to mention Christ), when
> their focus for change is on what the State can
> accomplish instead of the church locally embodying that
> change, when their energies are spent electing one
> candidate vs. another instead of on the ministries at their
> church, and when they find their time spent at their local
> church less than time spent reading news about the
> State/election/parties or working for political change.

> Patriotism is idolatrous when our hope is in the State and
> when our "agent" of change is the State, or the election
> and a specific candidate.

> Patriotism becomes idolatrous when our politic becomes
> State and not Church.

> For the follower of Jesus, the hope of the world is Jesus
> Christ and his embodiment in the Church, the People of
> Jesus (McKnight, "Converting our Imagination 6").

Historically, the warnings to the church are obvious. The problem is not that the church and the nation cannot work together, but that is not the primary way in which the church should be political. When that happens the church loses its unique identity as God's nation in this world and its witness becomes irrelevant. Since the fourth century, the political job description of the church has been reversed, with the politics of nation state power being primary for Christians and witness being secondary. But it is that agenda that has seriously undermined the church's witness. Is it any wonder that George Barna's research revealing that the way of life for Christians in the West is basically no different from their non-Christian neighbors? Once the state functionally takes the place of the church, there is no need for a distinctively Christian way of life, there is no need for a distinctively Christian witness.

The Christian moral life is reduced to nothing deeply profound; it is an ethic reduced in substance to nothing greater than being nice to our neighbors. But if the church can recover the politics of witness as its primary political task, then its alliances with the nation will have to be severely qualified and the way of life of the followers of Jesus will have to stand out as an alternative to the world and its ways. If not, its witness will be ineffective.

THE CHRISTENDOM CONTEXT

I think the reason that the politics of witness is so difficult for many Christians to engage with and understand is because for many centuries now the church in the West has been immersed in the Christendom context, where the mission of the church is conflated into the responsibilities of the state. In other words, church and state have been wedded together for so long that Christians have no idea how to think about politics apart from the nation. Whether it is a Constantinianism that seeks to enlist the state directly in fulfilling its agenda or a deceptive Enlightenment understanding of the separation of church and state that seeks to define religion as nothing more than a means for commending status quo morality that makes for good citizens, Christians in the West have been in this Christendom context for so long it is hard to think of the church's politics as something with its own integrity apart from the nations of the world.

Nowhere have I found this to be so obvious in the responses I receive when I put forward this robust political ecclesiology. The first response I hear is something along the lines of "Well, the church has by and large failed in its mission, and so we must rely on the state to achieve the necessary goals of justice and fairness and to provide for basic needs (e.g. health care)."

My response to this is two-fold. First, it's never been the church's place to provide for the needs of everyone. Christians are to do good to all, to be sure, but to think that the church's task is to meet everyone's basic needs is to lose the mission of the church

Jesus gave to it. Of course, that the mission of the church has been lost should not be surprising in a Christendom context where the politics of witness has been seriously compromised.

We must not forget Paul's words to the Galatians, "So then, whenever we have an opportunity, let us work for the good of all, and especially for those of the family of faith" (6:10). Paul is not suggesting that we ignore those outside of the Christian community. When he admonishes the Galatians to do good especially to those in the church he is providing the means by which the church can provide a witness to the world and the nations what God expects of them. For example, if individual churches would do what is necessary to provide basic health insurance for those in each congregation that had none, what a powerful witness that would be to the nation as well as the private sector. Such an approach would highlight the significance of the gospel in our just concerns for other believers' health instead of undermining the church's witness as Christians supported backroom deals behind closed doors on Capitol Hill and special exemptions in the form of payoffs to secure votes for a health care bill. Because Christians are immersed in Christendom, they think nothing of resorting to utilitarian arguments in order to support questionable moral behavior in achieving a just end. Just as St. Augustine and Eusebius in the fifth century did, Christians appealed to the ethic of pagans to justify the bad behavior of Christian politicians. Jesus' upside down kingdom ethic went by the wayside. In the end, how Christian did believers on both sides of the aisle appear during that debate? The word "Christian" is not a term I would use.

I need to state that I favor health care reform, although I am not convinced that what was passed in 2010 is very efficient or cost effective. Time, of course, will tell. But what I do oppose are Christians behaving badly, using power and coercion and political bribery in order to get the ends they think are just.

Second, the response that the church's failure is an excuse to embrace Christendom is tantamount to saying that the modern church can no longer follow the ecclesiology put forth by the writers of the New Testament and therefore its claims are no longer authoritative for us. Many years ago Reinhold Niebuhr argued that The Sermon on the Mount was an irrelevant ethic for a modern world with nation states which Christians now had a stake in maintaining (Niebuhr, *An Interpretation of Christian Ethics*, pp. 55-56). I would suggest that those who embrace Christendom as the best workable solution in the twenty-first century are saying the same thing in reference to the ecclesiology of the New Testament writers. They are suggesting that Paul's view of the church (and the other New Testament writers as well) is great if we could have listened, but since we have had seventeen centuries doing church another way in concert with the nations, it is best to leave the New Testament behind on this one and try to be the church as best as we can in our context. Our situation is simply too complex for the quaint theological musings of the New Testament. The religious right and the religious left place the first century church in the same category as Niebuhr did with Jesus—the category of irrelevance. They don't need the church when it comes to politics. The nation is their church.

I think another reason many Christians struggle with the politics of witness is that ultimately they like the idea of having power to make a difference. I am not suggesting by this that the religious right and the religious left have nefarious motives. These persons truly desire to affect positive change in their communities and in the world. But in their embracing of Christendom, they clearly run into conflict with the New Testament witness of Jesus and the upside down kingdom (Mark 10:35-45) and of Paul's commendations on the imitation of Christ (Philippians 2:1-11). It's not that the religious right and the religious left overtly reject these teachings, but they must reinterpret them to refer to how individual Christians must relate to one another or how the church should conduct its board meetings. No thought can be given to the possibility that in such passages we have a model for how the church must relate to the nations. Anyone familiar with the politics of the world knows that those with the power are not at the bottom, nor will humility and looking to the interests of others (and not those of one's constituency) bring much exaltation from others. In Christendom, Christian politics on the left and on the right looks no different from the politics of any old atheist.

We must recover the politics of witness.

MY (NOT SO) MODEST PROPOSAL

I have referred to this as a (not so) modest proposal because what I suggest is, I think, very basic. But given the permeating nature of Christendom in the church, it is a proposal that will be difficult to embrace. This proposal is a sketch. I am not laying out anything in detail. But I put it forth for further discussion.

First, I propose that the politics of witness will only work if the church at large and Christians as individuals live a simpler lifestyle. Materialism has all but destroyed the church's ability to witness politically in this world. It is not so much that the church lacks resources to fulfill its mission in this world, as it has too much of its resources tied up in things that, as Jesus himself said, "rot away" (Matthew 6:19). Churches are dumping resources into old run-down buildings, and individual Christians are in just as much debt as the average American. The problem is not that we lack financial resources; it's rather that they are tied up as a result of greed and an indistinguishable way of life. We cannot witness to the world by doing good to those of the household of faith if we cannot afford to assist those of the household of faith. Individual congregations need to live simply in order to feed their sisters and brothers in need and to provide health care for fellow Christians (one example) who do not have it. Moreover, Christians can and are forming health insurance co-operatives that are serving as examples of what true health care reform might look like—something that covers basic needs but has built-in cost controls that government run health insurance can never seem to contain. (For an example of such a co-op, see http://www.chministries.org/.) No, these co-ops are not perfect, but then nothing is. If enough individual churches could accomplish this in a general and consistent way, it would be a powerful model for the government and the private sector as to what both working together might be able to accomplish.

There should be no more generous people than the followers of Jesus. The politics of witness will only be effective when the church commits itself to living a simpler and more generous way of life. It is true that the church's resources are not unlimited, but it is just as true that the church is sitting on a gold mine of financial resources that cannot be used because the mine has caved in from massive debt and misplaced priorities.

Second, for the politics of witness to be effective Christians must not align themselves with political parties. To do so continues to undermine the politics of the kingdom and give normative status to the false modern political distinctions of left and right, conservative and liberal. Many years ago I heard George Hunter say that both the Democratic and Republican Parties needed to have Christians to hold both accountable. At one time I agreed with Hunter, but no longer. I have come to see that the only people that Christians in the Democratic Party want to hold accountable are Republicans. And the only persons that Christians in the Republican Party put under scrutiny are the Democrats. Thus, what indeed happens is exactly the opposite of what Hunter desires—Christians who identify with the Democratic Party identify more with non-christians who share their politics than with Christians who don't. The same, of course, is true with those Christians on the Republican side of the political aisle. Indeed, for those of us who spend any time reading Christian blogs where politics is discussed, the posts and subsequent comments do not concern the politics of the Kingdom per se, but the politics of left and right. Indeed, as one reads through the discussion, one wonders what is specifically Christian about the debate. Even posts specifically on the politics of the kingdom often move exclusively to the politics of right and left.

I have come to believe that as long as we believers identify and line up too closely with one side or the other, with either the

Republican Party or the Democratic Party, Christians will unintentionally eclipse the politics of God's kingdom and our prophetic voice and witness as the church will be undermined if not completely muted. Hunter's suggestion that Christians should join both political parties to hold them accountable sounds good, but in the final analysis those Christian individuals who do so, while well-meaning and sincerely motivated for the good, end up being the tools of the party they have joined. The politics of God's kingdom must know nothing of political parties.

The only way out of this conundrum is for Christians to distance themselves from such political group think. For those Christians who may involve themselves in the politics of the nation (and I believe there is a place for that), one would argue that lack of political party affiliation will all but destroy any Christian's chances of getting elected. Perhaps that is true, but the ends never justify the means. And if a church movement away from political parties were to gain serious momentum, who knows what is possible? But even if Christians with no major party affiliation find the nation state political drama to be a difficult climb uphill, it must be remembered that the church is where God's political kingdom action resides. The community of the cross is God's politics in this world.

Third, a Christian's call to the politics of the nation must be confirmed by the church just as much as the call to ordained ministry. The politics of witness does not deny that God may call individuals to be a witness in the halls of Congress. For those who think such involvement is important, why would they trivialize the politics of the nation by not testing a Christian's call to such politics? There isn't a church denomination that would simply ordain someone to ministry who felt called without resorting to a process of discernment to affirm or deny that call. And yet, we think nothing of the kind when it comes to a Christian's call to nation state politics. Politics is a dangerous and seductive business. The church has a stake in discerning whether or not certain individuals have the gifts and graces for such work, including the moral fortitude. For the church to confirm the call to nation state politics would also be a reminder that the church's authority is determinative and central for the believer and not the state.

Fourth, the politics of witness can probably only begin to happen in small enclaves of Christians who desire to be such a faithful remnant. It is true that where the church is growing in the world, its growth is primarily in the house church. I am not suggesting that Christians leave their large congregations to form smaller ones (though in some instances that might be appropriate), but I am saying that it is quite unlikely that any established congregation will be willing and therefore able to undertake such a (not so) modest proposal. We mainline Protestants like to think that we embrace the radical gospel of Jesus, but in reality we are into Christendom up to our ecclesiological armpits. For those individuals who find themselves in such a context and who desire to live out in their lives the politics of witness, they may have to find a remnant of faithful mainliners who will live out that witness in a small community setting while remaining faithful to their denominational church. Such a group would not only bear witness to the nation, but to the church so lost in Christendom that it doesn't even know it.

This list is not complete, and what has been mentioned needs further explication, but it is a start. I am sure that some who are reading this are probably wondering what the politics of witness has to do with the gospel. Isn't the first task of the church to make disciples of Jesus Christ? The short answer is yes, and we should be singularly focused on that task. But we will have a hard time convincing others of the truth of the gospel when Christians live a way of life that looks no different from anyone else and when we engage in the status quo politics of the nations of the world and refuse to live lives of simplicity in order to be generous toward the true needs of others.

This is not withdrawal from the world, nor is it the promotion of a sectarian ecclesiology. Such conclusions continue to assume that the nations of the world are calling the shots and the main political action takes place in the nations' capitals. But the politics of witness puts the church at the center of the action because it is God and not the nations who rules the world.

We are Jesus' witnesses in this world. It's about time the church recovered its true politics.

For Further Reading

Beckwith, Francis. *Politics for Christians: Statecraft as Soulcraft*, Downers Grove, IL: IVP Academic, 2010.

Bevere, Allan R. *All Is Not As It Seems Random Reflections on Faith, Ethics, and Politics.* Charleston: BookSurge, 2009.

Bevere, Allan R. *The Character of Our Discontent: Old Testament Portraits for Contemporary Times.* Gonzalez FL: Energion, 2010.

Bevere, Allan R. *Sharing in the Inheritance: Identity and the Moral Life in Colossians.* New York: Sheffield, 2003.

Black, David Alan. *Christian Archy.* Areopagus Critical Christian Issues, Vol. I. Gonzalez: FL: Energion, 2009.

Black, David Alan. *The Jesus Paradigm.* Gonzalez FL: Energion, 2009.

Boyd, Gregory. *The Myth of a Christian Nation: How the Quest for Political Power Is Destroying the Church.* Grand Rapids: Zondervan, 2006.

Carter, Craig. *Rethinking Christ and Culture: A Post-Christendom Perspective.* Grand Rapids: Brazos Press, 2007.

Eller, Vernard. *Christian Anarchy.* Eugene, OR: Wipf and Stock, 1999.

Ellul, Jacque. *The Subversion of Christianity.* Grand Rapids: Eerdmans, 1986.

Harink, Douglas. "God's Politics? A Response to Jim Wallis (Part One)." http://faith-theology.blogspot.com/2008/07/gods-politics-response-to-jim-wallis.html.

Harink, Douglas, "God's Politics? A Response to Jim Wallis (Part Two)." http://faith-theology.blogspot.com/2008/07/gods-politics-response-to-jim-wallis_30.html.

Hauerwas, Stanley. *Against the Nations: War and Survival in a Liberal Society.* Minneapolis: Winston, 1985.

Hauerwas, Stanley. *Dispatches from the Front: Theological Engagements with the Secular.* Durham: Duke University Press, 1995.

Hauerwas, Stanley. *Hannah's Child: A Theologian's Memoir.* Grand Rapids: Eerdmans, 2010.

Hauerwas, Stanley. *In Good Company: The Church as Polis.* (Notre Dame: University of Notre Dame Press, 1995.

Hauerwas, Stanley and William H. Willimon. *Resident Aliens: Life in the Christian Colony.* Nashville: Abingdon, 1989.

Hauerwas, Stanley and William H. Willimon. *Where Resident Alien Aliens Live: Exercises for Christian Practice.* Nashville: Abingdon, 1996.

Hunter, James. *To Change the World: The Irony, Tragedy, and Possibility of Christianity in the late Modern World.* Oxford: Oxford University Press, 2010.

Isaacson, Walter. *Benjamin Franklin: An American Life.* New York: Simon and Schuster, 2004.

Jones, L. Gregory (ed. *et al) God, Truth, and Witness: Engaging Stanley Hauerwas.* Grand Rapids: Brazos Press, 2005.

Kierkegaard, Søren, *Provocations.* New York: Orbis, 2002.

LaSor, William, David Hubbard, and Frederic Bush, *Old Testament Survey: The Message, Form, and Background of the Old Testament.* Grand Rapids: Eerdmans, 1982).

MacIntyre, Alasdair, *Whose Justice? Which Rationality?* Notre Dame: University of Notre Dame Press, 1989.

McKnight, Scot, "Converting Our Imagination 6." http://www.patheos.com/community/jesuscreed/?s=politics+church/.

McKnight, Scot. "A Second Take." http://www.patheos.com/community/jesuscreed/2010/10/18/a-second-take/.

Mapp, Alf. *The Faiths of Our Founders: What America's Founders Really Believed.* New York: Barnes & Noble, 2003.

Merrill, Dean. *Sinners in the Hands of an Angry Church.* Grand Rapids: Zondervan, 1997.

Niebuhr, Reinhold. *An Interpretation of Christian Ethics.* New York: Harper, 1935.

Penner, Archie. *The Christian, the State, and the New Testament.* Scottsdale: Herald Press, 1959.

Stassen, Glen H. and David P. Gushee, *Kingdom Ethics: Following Jesus in Contemporary Context.* Downers Grove: InterVaristy Press, 2003.

Stringfellow, William. *An Ethic for Christians and Other Aliens in a Strange Land*. Eugene, OR: Wipf and Stock, 2004.

Trible, Phyllis. "The Book of Jonah." *The New Interpreter's Bible: The Twelve Prophets*. Nashville, Abingdon, 1996.

Wallis, Jim. *God's Politics: Why the Right Gets It wrong and the Left Doesn't Get It*. San Francisco: Harper, 2005.

Wright, Tom. *The Original Jesus: the Life and Vision of a Revolutionary*. Grand Rapids: Eerdmans, 1996.

Yoder, John Howard. *Christian Attitudes to War, Peace, and Revolution: A Companion to Bainton*. Elkhart: Co-Op Bookstore, 1983. See now the readily available updated and edited version, John Howard Yoder, *Christians Attitudes toward War, Peace, and Revolution* (Theodore Koontz and Andy Alexis-Baker, eds.) Grand Rapids: Brazos Press, 2009.

Yoder, John Howard. *The Politics of Jesus: Vicit Agnus Noster*. Grand Rapids Eerdmans, 1972.

Topics and Persons Index

Abraham (also Abram)............ 5ff.
Adams, John............................. 29
American identity..................... 38
Anabaptists............................... 28
Atheism..................................... 31
Augustine...................... 19, 22, 56
Barna, George........................... 54
Beckwith, Francis..................... 44
Bevere, Allan R...................... 6, 8
Bishop Ambrose........................ 18
Black, David Alan..................... 46
Book of Common Prayer........ 32
Book of Nature......................... 32
Boyd, Gregory........................... 44
Calvin, John.............................. 29
Catholicism............................... 29
Chosenness.................................. 9
Christendom......xiff., 1, 3, 34, 51,
55ff., 61
Christian identity................. 34, 38
Christian left........38, 39, 46ff., 58
Christian right............. 38, 47f., 58
Christianity.... 1, 23, 27f., 33f., 36,
38, 48, 51
Doctrines of.....27ff., 33f., 36
Progressive........................ 45
Church..... 3, 17, 19f., 35, 40f., 49,
54, 61
And America...................... 53
And call............................. 60f.
And culture........................ 34
And empire.................. 18, 20f.
And Empire......... 18f., 22, 24
And Israel.................. 2, 5, 36
And political activism........ 43

And politics...... xiv, 2, 33, 49,
51f., 57
And state...2, 17, 19, 21, 23f.,
30, 33f., 48, 52f., 55, 57
And the nations................. 57
And the world.................... 23
As culture........................... 35
As nation............................ 36
As the people of God....... 38
Attendance........................ 30f.
Character of.............. xii, 1, 17
Community................... 13, 20
Discernment of................. 20
Distinctiveness of............ 22f.
Domestication of.............. 33
Failure of............................ 56
History of................... xiii, 15
House................................. 61
Identity of................ 22f., 53f.
Invisible...................... 21f., 25
Mainline............................. 45
Marginalized.... 2, 34, 40f., 57
Mission of. xiif., 19, 22ff., 36,
38, 51, 53ff., 61
Patriotic worship services in. 38
Paul's view of.................... 57
Politically invisible............. 35
Politics of.. xiif., 3, 15, 17, 20,
52, 55, 57, 60, 62
Purpose of................... 31, 35
Resources.......................... 58f.
Role of... 35, 40f., 47f., 55, 59
True.................................... 21
Visible............................. 20ff.
Witness of....... xii, 2f., 19, 24,
40f., 46ff., 54ff., 58, 60, 62
Cicero... 18

Civil religion............................ 37ff.

Constantine.....xiii, 2f., 17ff., 24f.,
            27, 33, 36, 49

Constantinian Shift.... 17, 20, 22f.

Constantinianism. xiii, 1, 34ff., 55

Constitutional Convention.......32

Council of Constantinople...... 19

Council of Nicaea..................... 18

Deism............................ 28, 31, 34

Democratic Party.....3, 43, 45, 47,
                                    59f.

Disciples, Twelve.................... 1, 12

Dobson, James............................47

Double-predestination..............29

Ecclesiology..................................
            General..................xii, 21, 56
            New Testament................. 57
            Political.............. xii, 41, 51, 55
            Radically reshaped..............19
            Sectarian............................. 61
            Status quo..........................xiii

Election, Doctrine of.............. 31

Ellul, Jacques............................ xi

Emperor Theodosius.............. 19

Enlightenment.....2, 24, 27f., 33f.,
                                  36, 55

Eusebius......................... 19, 22, 56

Evangelical left.................. 38, 45

Ezra..9

Falwell, Jerry........................ 39, 45

Franklin, Benjamin...... 2, 25, 27f.,
                                    31ff.

Gentiles........................9, 11ff., 24

Gospel..................................34, 53

Gushee, David....................... 43

Harink, Douglas..................... 53f.

Hauerwas, Stanley..xi, xiii, 22, 35,
                                        37

Health care reform.............56, 58

Health insurance.................56, 58

Holy Roman Empire................22

Hunter, James..x, 37ff., 43ff., 59f.

Idolatry.....................................8f.

Isaacson, Walter........................ 32

Israel......1, 5, 7ff., 15, 22, 37f., 40
            And America................ 37, 39
            And the church.......... 2, 5, 36
            And the Church.............. 37f.
            Call of.......................... 6, 8, 11
            Reconstitution of...............12

James (apostle).................. 14, 23f.

Jefferson, Thomas......2, 25, 27ff.,
                                    33f., 36

Jesus, Politics of............. 15, 23, 52

John (apostle)..................... 14, 23f.

Jonah................................... 10f.

King George III.........................31

Kingdom..............................
            Of God......24, 40, 46, 48, 50
            Politics of............. 48, 50, 59f.

Kingdom living........................... 52

LaSor, William........................9

Leithart, Peter......................xiii

Lohfink, Gerhard.......................1

Madison, James....................... 28

Mainline Protestants.................61

Mapp, Alf................................. 29

Materialism........................41, 58

McIntyre, Alasdair.................... 47

McKnight, Scot................51f., 54

Merrill, Dean................... 27f., 41

New Testament......20, 22, 35, 40,
                                43, 49, 51, 57

Niebuhr, Reinhold.................... 57

Old Testament..... 6, 9, 11, 18, 38,
                                  40, 44

Original sin............................... 29

Paul... 29

Political process........................ 51

Politics...
            Kingdom..............................3
            Left................................... 59
            Nation state..........................2

Power.................2, 14, 43f., 53
Right.......................................59
Pollitt, Katha.............................. 45
Priestly, Joseph............................ 29
Protestant Reformers.................28
Religious left..... 2, 37ff., 43ff., 49,
                                         53, 57
Religious right...2, 37ff., 43ff., 49,
                                         53, 57
Reprobation, Doctrine of.........31
Republican Party xi, 3, 43, 47, 59f.
Resurrection.. 14f., 21, 24, 28, 30,
                                         33f., 48
Robertson, Pat..................... 39, 45
Roman Empire.................... 17, 41
Sarah (also Sarai)...................... 5ff.
Sermon on the Mount.. 5, 22, 24,
                                         46f., 57
Stassen, Glen............................. 43

State....... xiii, 1f., 17, 19, 21ff., 28,
            33ff., 39ff., 48f., 52ff., 60f.
     And church.............. 30, 55
     Modern................................ 35
     Power of............................. 40
     Secular.................................44
Stringfellow, William.................. xi
Tertullian....................................... 41
Trible, Phyllis.............................. 10
Wallis, Jim...............38f., 45, 47, 53
Willimon, William H................. 35
Witness...
     Christian............................. 54
     Politics of... xiff., 17, 25, 40f.,
                         48ff., 55f., 58ff.
Wright, N. T....................... 5, 7, 13
Yoder, John Howard...... xi, xiiiff.,
                                         17ff.

Scripture Index

Genesis 12:1-9................................6
Deuteronomy 30:19................. 39
2 Chronicles 7:14.................38, 41
Ezra 9:1-5..................................10
Ezra 9:12-15............................ 10
Ezra 10:19, 44.......................... 10
Isaiah 10:1-2............................ 39
Isaiah 10:1-19........................... 52
Isaiah 51:1-6................................7
Isaiah 60.................................... 7
Isaiah 60:1-5...............................7
Isaiah 65:20-25........................ 45
Amos 1:2-2:3........................... 40
Micah 4:1-4............................... 45
Micah 6:8...................................41
Matthew 2:34-40...................... 39

Matthew 5:14-16...................... 51
Matthew 6:19............................58
Mark 10:35-37.......................... 14
Mark 10:35-45.....................23, 57
Mark 10:42-45.......................... 13
Mark 12:1-12........................... 13
Mark 13:10................................15
John 8:32................................... 39
John 17:20-21........................... 34
Romans 12................................23
Romans 13................................23
1 Corinthians 15:16-19............. 34
Galatians 6:10............................56
Colossians 2:14........................ 24
Colossians 3...............................34

Also by Allan R. Bevere

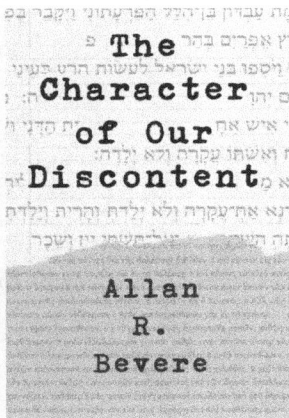

The Character of Our Discontent

Allan R. Bevere

The Character of Our Discontent grew out of the author's conviction that pastors do not preach enough about the Old Testament. The result is 19 chapters, each of which represents a sermon on an Old Testament character. These sermons are lively, fast paced, and practical yet are rooted in sound scholarship and are examples of the homiletical art.

Christians who would like to learn how the Old Testament can enlighten and guide their Christian walk, and pastors who would like to learn how to preach more effectively from the Old Testament will both find these sermons an invaluable aid.

Also in the
Areopagus Critical Christian Issues Series

What is the Kingdom of God? What does it mean to be part of the kingdom? These are questions that should occupy the mind of every Christian. But we frequently shy away from the full meaning of God's rule.

In *Christian Archy*, **Dr. David Alan Black** examines the New Testament to find the truly radical and all-encompassing claims of God's kingdom. In doing so, he discovers that the character of this kingdom is widely different from what is commonly contemplated today. Its glory is revealed only through suffering — a point that Jesus' disciples, then and now, have been slow to understand. This truth has tremendous implications for church life. The kingdom of God is in no way imperialistic. It has no political ambitions. It conquers not by force but by love. It is this humble characteristic of the kingdom that is a stumbling block to so many today. Christ's claim to our total allegiance is one we seek to avoid at all costs. But there is only one way to victory and peace, and that way is the way of the Lamb.

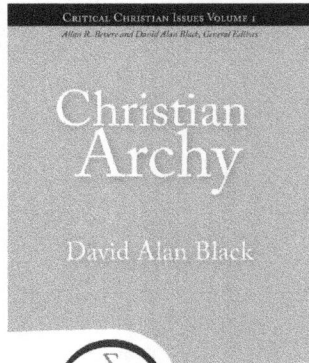

CRITICAL CHRISTIAN ISSUES VOLUME 1
Allan R. Bevere and David Alan Black, General Editors

Christian Archy

David Alan Black

Σ
AREOPAGUS
CRITICAL CHRISTIAN ISSUES

More from Energion Publications

Personal Study

The Jesus Paradigm	$17.99
Finding My Way in Christianity	$16.99
When People Speak for God	$17.99
Holy Smoke, Unholy Fire	$14.99
Not Ashamed of the Gospel	$12.99
Evidence for the Bible	$16.99
Christianity and Secularism	$16.99
What's In A Version?	$12.99
Christian Archy	$9.99
Ultimate Allegiance	$9.99

Christian Living

Daily Devotions of Ordinary People – Extraordinary God	$19.99
Directed Paths	$7.99
Grief: Finding the Candle of Light	$8.99
I Want to Pray	$7.99
Soup Kitchen for the Soul	$12.99

Bible Study

Learning and Living Scripture	$12.99
To the Hebrews: A Participatory Study Guide	$9.99
Revelation: A Participatory Study Guide	$9.99
The Gospel According to St. Luke: A Participatory Study Guide	$8.99
Identifying Your Gifts and Service: Small Group Edition	$12.99
Consider Christianity, Volume I & II Study Guides	$7.99 each
The Character of Our Discontent	$12.99
Why Four Gospels?	$11.99

Theology

God's Desire for the Nations	$18.99
Out of This World: An Assessment of Christian Community	$24.99

Generous Quantity Discounts Available

Dealer Inquiries Welcome

Energion Publications

P.O. Box 841

Gonzalez, FL 32560

Website: http://energionpubs.com

Phone: (850) 525-3916